YORK NOTES

Alfred, Lord Tennyson
Selected Poems

Note by Glennis Byron

 Longman   York Press

The right of Glennis Byron to be identified as Author of this Work has been
asserted by her in accordance with the Copyright, Designs and Patents Act 1988

YORK PRESS
322 Old Brompton Road, London SW5 9JH

PEARSON EDUCATION LIMITED
Edinburgh Gate, Harlow,
Essex CM20 2JE, United Kingdom
Associated companies, branches and representatives throughout the world

First published 2000
15 14 13 12

ISBN: 978-0-582-42483-8

Designed by Vicki Pacey
Phototypeset by Gem Graphics, Trenance, Mawgan Porth, Cornwall
Colour reproduction and film output by Spectrum Colour
Printed in China
EPC/12

CONTENTS

PART ONE

INTRODUCTION

HOW TO STUDY A POEM

Studying on your own requires self-discipline and a carefully thought-out work plan in order to be effective.

- First, learn to hear it: say it aloud, silently, whenever you read it. The poem lives in its sounds; poetry is as close to music and dance as it is to prose.
- A poem is not reducible to what you can extract from it at the end of the process of interpretation; it is a dramatic event, a *sequence* of thoughts and emotions.
- The only true summary of the poem is the poem. What can be summarised is one's experience of the poem, the process by which one arrives at a reading.
- What is the poem's tone of voice? Who is speaking?
- Does the poem have an argument? Is it descriptive?
- Is there anything special about the poem's language? Which words stand out? Why?
- What elements are repeated? Consider **alliteration**, **assonance**, **rhyme**, rhythm, **metaphor**.
- What might the poem's images suggest or **symbolise**? Do they fit together thematically?
- Is there a regular pattern of lines? Are they **end-stopped** (where the grammatical units coincide with line endings) or does the phrasing 'run over'?
- Can you compare and contrast the poem with other work by the same poet?
- Finally, every argument you make about the poem must be backed up with details and quotations. Always express your ideas in your own words.

This York Note offers an introduction to the poetry of Tennyson and cannot substitute for close reading of the text and the study of secondary sources.

Tennyson's first collection of poetry, *Poems, Chiefly Lyrical*, appeared in 1830, seven years before Victoria ascended the throne. He died in 1892, only nine years before the queen. His work spanned the age, and for the Victorians, Alfred, Lord Tennyson, Poet Laureate, became as much an emblem of the era as Victoria herself. He was the first poet ever to become a popular public figure. Anticipating the way modern visitors might take a tour of the stars' homes in Hollywood or visit Elvis's Graceland, many Victorians made pilgrimages to his home on the Isle of Wight, peering into the gardens in the hope of a glimpse of their idol. Tennyson's lyrics were set to music and sung in drawing-rooms around the country. Significantly, his was one of the three English voices (the others were those of Victoria, who refused, and Gladstone) that Thomas Edison wanted to record on his phonograph; he was the representative voice of the age, the voice of an empire.

Tennyson can still speak to, and even, in a rather interesting way, *for*, us today. Those who never read poetry might recognise and quote, without knowing the source, such lines as 'Nature red in tooth and claw', 'Kind hearts are more than coronets', ''tis better to have loved and lost than never to have loved at all' or 'In the spring a young man's fancy lightly turns to thoughts of love'. There are few other writers, perhaps only Shakespeare, whose poetry has entered into the common language in such a vital and enduring way.

In literary studies, Tennyson remains equally important, although we are no longer so quick to identify him as the straightforward spokesperson for Victorian middle-class values. Tennyson himself once said that 'every reader must find his own interpretation according to his ability, and according to his sympathy with the poet' (Hallam Tennyson, *Alfred Lord Tennyson: A Memoir*, 1897, vol. 2. p. 127). To that we should add that our interpretations of Tennyson will also be influenced by the knowledge, the concerns and even the reading strategies of our own age. We still recognise Tennyson's close association with his world; indeed, we see Tennyson as being, in the words of Eve Sedgwick, 'a Christmas present to the twentieth-century student of ideology' (in Rebecca Stott, ed., *Tennyson*, Longman, 1996, p.182). But we are not looking, as the Victorians were, for a spokesperson for the dominant values of the age, and, with the distance imposed by time, we are more able to recognise that Tennyson's relationship with his times was much more problematic than his contemporary readers believed. Critics like Alan Sinfield now see Tennyson as engaged in a struggle with the dominant ideology, questioning the values of a materialist and capitalistic world and conventional middle-class thinking with respect to gender and sexuality. We also now believe, however, that it is exactly all this questioning that makes Tennyson so typically Victorian.

In a world of unprecedented change, when all absolute values in spiritual, moral and social matters were constantly being undermined, the Victorians had little confidence in general fixed truths and questioning was an inevitable response. In this respect it is particularly significant that the main innovation in poetic form during the Victorian age was the **dramatic monologue**, a form which emphasises the subjective, historical, relative nature of truth, and which, through the interaction of poet, speaker, auditor and reader, accommodates a plurality of perspectives. In attempting to assess Tennyson's position with respect to the ideology of his age, therefore, we should be wary of conflating the poet with his dramatic **personas**; this is something about which Tennyson himself was continually reminding his readers. When one reviewer solemnly warned, with respect to *Maud*: 'If an author pipe of adultery, fornication, murder and suicide, set him down as the practiser of these crimes', Tennyson was quick to respond: 'Adulterer I may be, fornicator I may be, murderer I may be, suicide I am not yet' (quoted in Robert Bernard Martin, *Tennyson. The Unquiet Heart*, Clarendon, 1980, pp. 390–1).

Tennyson's poetry is not only of interest for what it can reveal to us about his age; we are still very much the children of the Victorians and many of their concerns remain ours. We still share Tennyson's interest in psychology, in the way in which the self is so much a construct of the society in which it emerges; we are still troubled by questions of gender and sexuality, by empire building and by war, by the relationship between humanity and the environment. Tennyson's poetry also offers much to delight the modern reader who can appreciate both the visual pictures he creates and the wide range of sound effects he produces. He is one of the most successful of all poets at conveying abstract ideas through concrete and vividly pictorial language; it is no wonder that so many artists have been inspired to translate scenes from such poems as 'The Lady of Shalott' into a visual medium. The best way of appreciating the varied sound effects of his poetry is to read it aloud; Tennyson himself was rather fond of doing this in the company of his friends; he had a grand deep voice which swayed onwards in a long drawn out chant, a voice which Elizabeth Barrett Browning described as like an organ. Something of this can still be detected in the recordings he made near the end of his life on Edison's wax cylinders. Despite the primitive quality of the recording and the age of the wax cylinders before the sounds were transferred on to modern discs, hints of the power of his voice still emerge out of the distorting background noises. It is appropriate that a poet who continues to have so much to say to us today can still, literally, be heard.

PART TWO

COMMENTARIES

Tennyson published his first poetry in 1827: Poems by Two Brothers *included poems by him, his brother Charles, and a few by his brother Frederick. This was soon followed by* Poems, Chiefly Lyrical *(1830) and* Poems *(1832).* Poems *(1842) was released in two volumes: the first included a selection of poems from the 1832 edition, extensively revised.* The Princess: A Medley *appeared in 1847 and* In Memoriam A.H.H. *in 1850. The* Idylls of the King *was written and published in stages: the first four appeared in 1859, and the sequence was finally completed with the publication of 'Balin and Balan' in 1885. Other volumes include* Enoch Arden *(1864),* Ballads and Other Poems *(1880),* Tiresias and Other Poems *(1885),* Locksley Hall Sixty Years After *(1886),* Demeter and Other Poems *(1889) and, published posthumously,* The Death of Oenone, Akba's Dream and Other Poems *(1892).*

Tennyson also wrote a number of plays: Queen Mary *(1875),* Harold *(1876),* The Cup and the Falcon *(1884),* Becket *(1884),* The Promise of May *(1886), and* The Foresters *(1892). A complete edition of the* Works *was published by Hallam Tennyson (Eversley edition), 1907–8. The standard modern edition is Christopher Ricks's* The Poems of Tennyson *(1969), and the text used in this Note is the Penguin* Alfred Lord Tennyson: Selected Poems, *edited by Aidan Day. Poems selected for discussion have been chosen to give an indication of the range and development of Tennyson's poetry, but, because of his extensive output, some of the longer works have not been represented; in the case of* The Princess *only the songs and lyrics are analysed in detail. Poem titles in the following commentaries are followed by the date of first publication and, when appropriate, the date of publication in revised form.*

Quotations from the poems are identified by line number in parenthesis and, when necessary, by section number also.

Mariana (1830)

A description of an abandoned woman's state of consciousness

Amid the almost treeless landscape of the Fens, Mariana awaits her lover, who will never come again. The **epigraph** of the poem refers to the Mariana of Shakespeare's *Measure for Measure*, a woman who is deserted by her lover Angelo; however, there is no sense that Tennyson's Mariana will be reunited with her lover as she is in Shakespeare's play, or, indeed, some critics would suggest, that she would necessarily wish it.

Because the emphasis here is on description, the poem is almost impossible to summarise: nothing actually happens. The first eight lines of each **stanza** offer a description of either Mariana's home, the 'lonely moated grange' (line 8), or of Mariana herself. The final four lines of each stanza, the **refrain**, are spoken by the waiting Mariana, a woman abandoned by her lover, and convey her frustration, the dreariness of her life and her wish for death.

Although the grange where Mariana lives is described by an unknown narrator, it is described as Mariana sees it: she appears fused with her setting. Everything in the poem is a product of her mind; both the grange in which she lives and the surrounding landscape are ultimately little more than an emanation of her consciousness (see also Critical Approaches, on Language). The emphasis here is not on any action or event but on atmosphere: what is important is not so much the objects that are described, such as the shed, the moss, the nails, but the *effect* that these objects have. Appropriately then, the syntactical arrangement of sentences tends to emphasise adjectives, or descriptive words, over verbs, or action words. The overwhelming effect or feeling is one of stagnation. There are numerous images of decay, darkness and desolation. Even when Tennyson **personifies** elements of the setting, as in the sluice which 'with blacken'd waters slept' (line 38), the effect remains the same; there is little sense of active life here. The one potentially significant action is negated: 'He cometh not'. How, then, is time treated in the poem? Why is the clock slow, why does the cock sing 'an hour ere light' (line 27)? Time appears to be irrelevant in this world 'without hope of change' (line 29), without action. There is no sense of movement or progression; everything is static, coated in moss, dust or rust. The very house itself dreams.

If this is primarily a psychological landscape, then this suggests that Mariana too is held in stasis, obsessively dwelling upon the one thought 'He cometh not'. The world around her is level and monotonous, its flatness broken only by one poplar tree, in much the same way as Mariana has only one obsessive thought. The tree is also, some critics suggest, as tall and masculine as her departed lover, and so perhaps there is a hint of sexual frustration in the way the shadow of this poplar sways upon her curtain and falls 'upon her bed, across her brow' (line 56). But is it clear that Mariana would actually want that lover to return now, or is she in some sense happy in her frustration, her passion, her suffering? Harold Bloom has suggested that this is a deliciously unhealthy poem where the woman is too happy in her unhappiness to want anything more. Would you agree? Does Mariana really desire consummation? Interestingly, the one hour she loathes the most is the late afternoon when the sun sinks towards the horizon, and this could be associated with some kind of conclusion or completion. Alternately this is the ending of another day, and for Mariana time is something which has stopped, and, perhaps, something she wants to remain stopped; any indication of progression or movement is abhorrent. When the old voices call her from without, they seem to be a call to suicide, but even this would involve too much energy for Mariana.

How is the endlessly repetitive and static nature of Mariana's existence conveyed formally by the poem? This is at least partly achieved through the **rhyme** scheme (*ababcddcefef*), which evokes both stasis and enclosure. In the circling central **quatrain** the first and last lines enclose the middle two lines, while the framing quatrains serve to enclose this central quatrain as a whole. The last quatrain in each stanza always rhymes with the words 'dreary / said / aweary / dead', repeatedly bringing us back to the same point. The **assonance** and the unstressed endings make the rhyming words 'dreary' and 'aweary' seem drawn out and languorous. This effect is further emphasised by the way an extra unstressed syllable is added to the **iambic** line in 'aweary, aweary'. Repetition generally dominates the poem, and is most notable in the refrain that Mariana speaks (see Critical Approaches, on Sound Patterning). While there are slight variations, these generally only serve to emphasise the basic sameness of her thought. There are, however, more striking variations in the final stanza. The adverb shifts from 'only' to 'then', from 'He cometh not' to 'He will not come', and from 'I would that I were dead' to 'Oh God, that I were dead'. The overall effect is that Mariana appears more emphatic, more determined here. Perhaps this change is related to the fact that this is expressed at sunset, with all its suggestions of consummation or progression, both things Mariana appears anxious to avoid.

'Mariana in the moated grange' Shakespeare, *Measure for Measure*, III.1.2: 'There, at the moated grange, resides this dejected Mariana'
marish-mosses marsh moss

THE KRAKEN (1830)

A description of a sea monster

A wondrous sea monster, the Kraken, lies silent in a dreamless sleep until the day when the fires heat the sea and he will be seen once as he comes roaring to the surface and then dies.

Tennyson frequently uses the deep sea to represent what he calls, in 'The Palace of Art', 'the abysmal deeps of Personality' (line 223), and this quite puzzling poem is often read as a description of repressed, unconscious forces. Both the Kraken's habitat and the fact that he is asleep suggest this emphasis on inwardness. His existence is mindless; he is quite unaware of everything that goes on around him; he even feeds instinctively rather than consciously, 'battening upon huge seaworms in his sleep' (line 12). How does Tennyson formally suggest the changeless existence of this creature under the sea? The **rhyme** scheme could be said to contribute to a sense of monotony. Not only does deep / sleep return at the end of the lyric, but the **assonantal** 'ee' sound echoes throughout, with sea / flee / green / seen, while the 'ay' sound of the rhyming words height / light is echoed in another set of rhyming words polypi / lie / die.

The main problem in interpreting this poem lies in the final lines. Is this creature the embodiment of mindless repression and its final predicted rising to the surface a signal of release and transformation? If so, why is this followed immediately by death? In this respect the Kraken rather monstrously anticipates the Lady of Shalott who must also die once she leaves her isolated tower and engages with the outside world. The reference to when 'latter fire shall heat the deep' (line 13) may invite a Christian, apocalyptic reading; in Revelation, at the sound of the seven trumpets the world is purged and destroyed, partly by fire. As the second angel blows his trumpet, 'What looked like a great mountain flaming with fire was hurled into the sea' (Revelation 8:8). In a Christian reading, then, the poem could be interpreted as an anticipation of the end of the world.

THE LADY OF SHALOTT (1832; REV. 1842)

The Lady of Shalott is cursed to stay in her tower, weaving the sights she sees in her mirror. The appearance of Lancelot prompts her to turn and look directly upon the world. She leaves the tower and, as she floats down to Camelot in a boat, dies

Part 1 introduces the lady who is confined to her tower on the island of Shalott; she is never seen, but sometimes heard by the reapers in the fields. Part 2 takes us inside the castle and describes her activities. Weaving a magic web in which she reproduces what she sees through a mirror, she is prevented by some unspecified curse from directly viewing the world outside. The images she sees in her mirror are 'shadows of the world' (line 48), villagers, market girls, and knights and pages from Camelot, and yet she 'still delights' (line 64) in her weaving. But the juxtaposition of the funerals with 'two younger lovers lately wed' (line 70) seems to force her to recognise the sterility of her life: 'I am half sick of shadows' (line 71). In Part 3 the dazzling image of Sir Lancelot appears in the mirror, singing as he rides to Camelot; she springs up and moves

to the window to look. The web flies out, the mirror cracks, and the lady
cries 'The curse is come upon me' (line 116). Part 4 shows the lady
coming out of her tower, finding a boat, and writing her name on the
prow. She lies down in the boat and the stream takes her, singing her last
song, down to Camelot; before she arrives she dies. The people of
Camelot come down to see her and fearfully wonder who she is and what
has happened. Sir Lancelot muses upon her, observes the loveliness of her
face, and asks for God to 'lend her grace' (line 170).

> Part 1 establishes the setting and the context; in this description of
> the lady's world, is the overall effect negative or positive? She lives
> in a castle, **synecdochally** described as 'Four gray walls, and four
> gray towers' (line 15). This might suggest protection, but perhaps
> more clearly imprisonment. And yet these walls overlook 'a space of
> flowers' (line 16), and the island itself 'imbowers' (line 17) her,
> indicating an attractive, secure and comforting retreat. Then again,
> outside there is movement and freedom, while inside there is stasis
> and confinement. There is a heavy emphasis on the visual in this
> opening section, but the lady herself is never seen; the shallop floats
> by 'unhail'd' (line 21); she is never seen waving or even standing at
> her casement. She is known only as a voice. The opening, then, sets
> up an opposition between an isolated and secure world of
> withdrawal, associated with Shalott, and the social and active world
> which will be embodied primarily by Camelot. Do you think
> Tennyson creates a sense of repetitive sameness in this opening
> section or a sense of movement? The **rhyme** scheme (*aaaabcccb*)
> might seem to contribute to a feeling of sameness or stasis, along
> with the repetition of Camelot/Shalott. On the other hand, the
> constant rhyming of these words might create a sense of inevitable
> progression, a sense that the Lady is going to be driven onwards
> towards her unavoidable fate.
>
> Part 2 offers an explanation of what the lady does and why she is
> confined to the tower. What is the nature of the curse? Partly
> because of the various meanings which may be attached to 'stay',
> that is, to stop, or to remain in the same place, the nature of the
> curse can be seen as quite ambiguous; the lady has heard 'A curse is
> on her if she stay / To look down to Camelot' (line 40–1). This

could suggest that the curse will be on her if she stops her weaving and looks down, the most common reading of the lines. However, it might also suggest that if she stays, remains, in the tower, she will be cursed to look down to Camelot. Why do you think it is significant that she views the world only through a mirror? She sees nothing but reflections, or 'Shadows of the world' (line 48). The Lady is said to delight still in weaving the sights she sees, but by the end of this section she is claiming 'I am half sick of shadows' (line 71). What do you think has caused this? The line is preceded by a description of what she often sees in her mirror: funerals or lovers. By staying in her tower, she remains distanced from human relationships, from life itself.

Part 3 introduces the Lady's downfall. How do the descriptions of Lancelot contrast with the descriptions of the Lady? Suddenly, we are presented with a number of **similes**. He is presented in terms of dazzling images of vitality, bright lights, clanging sounds. The sun blazes upon him, his shield sparkles, his armour clashes and flashes, his bridle glitters, his brow glows. He flashes into the Lady's mirror 'From the bank and from the river' (line 105); he is reflected directly but there is also the reflection of his image on the water. For the first and only time in this poem, a word rhymes with itself 'river' / 'river', emphasising the idea of reflection. Just how real is the image of Lancelot that the Lady receives? Herbert Tucker suggests he is 'pure representation: a man of mirrors, a signifier as hollow as the song he sings' (*Tennyson and the Doom of Romanticism*, Harvard University Press, 1988, p.112). If the Lady is attracted by him, then, perhaps she is attracted by something that is illusory. In the fourth stanza of Part 3, there is a significant change in the **refrain**. Before this, the middle line of each stanza focuses upon either Camelot or Lancelot, while the last line of each stanza focuses upon Shalott and the Lady. This serves both to link and to separate Camelot and Shalott. At this crucial point in the poem, however, immediately before the Lady leaves the web to look out upon Camelot, Lancelot intrudes upon her space not only by becoming part of her world but also formally by taking over her place in the refrain, and the stanza ends with '"Tirra lirra," by the river / Sang Sir Lancelot' (lines 107–8). At this moment of crisis, the predominantly **trochaic** rhythms are replaced by resounding **iambs**, suggestive of the intensity of the Lady's desire to look: 'She left the web, she left the loom, / She made three paces thro' the room' (lines 109–10). The **anaphoric** repetition of 'she' along with the consistently repeated grammatical structure of the lines, gives further weight to the climactic moment. The sense of a driving movement onwards is heavily emphasised now.

In Part 4 of the poem, as the lady comes down from her tower and finds a boat, there is a sudden shift in the seasons; the 'blue unclouded weather' (line 91) of summer gives way to the storms and the dying of the 'pale yellow woods' (line 119); all these points stress the natural cycle in which the Lady has now become involved and anticipate her consequently inevitable death. As she has previously turned the world into an aesthetic image, now she does much the same for herself; 'robed in snowy white' (line 136) she takes a small boat and names her last production: '*The Lady of Shalott*' (line 126). Like the proverbial swan that sings before it dies, the Lady is heard 'singing her last song' (line 143). What do you think of Lancelot's ultimate response to the Lady? After he 'mused a little space' (line 168), he concludes 'She has a lovely face' (line 169). Considering that he has been the cause of her death, this might seem to us rather superficial, but then again, Lancelot is quite unaware of the role he has played.

Many critics have seen this as a poem about art itself, and certainly, with its insistent rhyme scheme and formal divisions, 'The Lady of Shalott' emphasises its status as a work of art. Furthermore, the lady herself is an artist, weaving pictures of the world. In this reading the relation between art and life is embodied in the worlds of Shalott and Camelot; life is seen as antipathetic to art: the artist must remain detached, not participating directly in life but viewing it through the mirror of the imagination. The curse thus becomes the inevitable condition of the artist's existence. The poem can more basically be read as an expression of the tension between the impulse towards life and the impulse towards death. Some critics consider the poem an expression of a conflict between a drive towards social commitment and a contrasting desire for autonomy, marked by scepticism about the viability of any social commitment in an unresponsive society. More recently, **Post-structuralist** critics have read the poem as an example of the reading process itself; **feminist critics** have suggested it concerns the enforced passivity of women and the movement from the private/feminine sphere to the public/masculine sphere; while **Marxist critics** have seen the poem to be about the estrangement of literary labour. Perhaps it is because the poem invites so many different readings that it has enjoyed a long popular appeal. The poem was a particular favourite of the **Pre-Raphaelite** artists, and you might find it interesting to look at some of the paintings of 'The Lady of Shalott' by such artists as Holman Hunt, Millais and Waterhouse.

shallop   light boat used for rowing in shallow water

greaves   leg armour

gemmy   covered in gems

baldric   sash or belt worn over right shoulder to the left hip, often used for carrying a sword; here it contains Lancelot's bugle

Tirra lirra   taken from Autolycus's song in Shakespeare's *The Winter's Tale*, IV.2.9; Autolycus is thinking of 'tumbling in the hay' with prostitutes

OENONE (1832; REV. 1842)

The nymph Oenone tells of her desertion by Paris and expresses her frustration and her desire for vengeance

The poem begins with a description of the landscape, establishing a distinction between the valley in Ida where Oenone lives and the city of Troy that is revealed in the distance.

Oenone, a mountain nymph and the daughter of a river-god, wanders into this valley, mournful and forlorn. The poem then dramatically changes its generic mode, moving from **idyll** to **monologue**, as Oenone begins to speak; she tells the story of her desertion by Paris, repeatedly calling upon Mount Ida to hear her before she dies. Paris, who has been living a carefree life as a shepherd, is actually the son of a king. Oenone recalls how Paris came to her with the apple from the garden of the Hesperides on which was engraven 'For the most fair'. He tells her it should be awarded to her, and that it was thrown down before the gods as they gathered in the halls of Peleus. Although Paris does not explain, it was thrown there by Eris, goddess of discord, who was angered by not being invited. Iris, the messenger of the gods, has given it to Paris, telling him he has been chosen to award the apple. Herè (Hera), Pallas Athene and Aphrodite all claim it belongs to them, and these three goddesses come naked to the bower where Paris must make his judgement. Herè offers him power and Paris is tempted, but Pallas Athene, angered, offers wisdom: 'self-reverence, self-knowledge, and self-control' (line 142), she claims, will alone lead to true power. Oenone urges Paris to award the apple to Pallas, but Aphrodite seductively draws near and offers him the 'fairest and most loving wife in Greece' (line 183). (This will be Helen, wife of Menelaus, and her subsequent abduction leads to the sack of Troy.) Paris chooses Aphrodite. In the remainder of her speech, Oenone bemoans the loss of Paris and recalls the devastation of her forest. She is full of 'fiery thoughts' (line 242) and these thoughts turn towards the future. She determines to go to talk with the prophetess Cassandra, who is haunted by a vision of fire and war. The final images of fire anticipate both the burning of Troy, of which Cassandra is warned, and Oenone's own eventual self-immolation on the funeral pyre of Paris.

'Oenone' is part idyll, part monologue, written in the **blank verse** that is so useful for suggesting speech. This is a stage in Tennyson's development of the **dramatic monologue** (see Critical Approaches, on Poetic Form, and Historical & Literary Background). What does the opening description of the landscape suggest about the valley where Oenone wanders and about the city of Troy? In the valley, the vapour 'slopes', 'creeps,' and 'loiters, slowly drawn' (lines 3–5). A sense of quiet and even stasis contrasts with the roar of the brook which falls to the sea. Troy itself, as we shall be aware, is conventionally associated with action, battle, and destruction. The opening, then, sets up the important opposition between the pastoral world and the doomed city. In what ways could we say Oenone's mood reflects the mood of the valley that has just been described? Whether she is 'wandering forlorn' (line 15) or 'leaning on a fragment' (line 19) she appears languorous, even listless. There is a sense of stasis here too. Oenone seems incapable of breaking out of her situation, breaking away from her obsessive dependence on

Paris, and, as her repeated refrain further implies, incapable of changing her lament. By the time she concludes her first stanza, with 'My eyes are full of tears, my heart of love, / My heart is breaking, and my eyes are dim, / And I am all aweary of my life' (lines 30–2), we may think that her lament is simply another version of the lament in Tennyson's 'Mariana'. But while Mariana seems totally self-absorbed, totally uninterested in communicating to another, Oenone is determined that she will be heard and her story told.

Once Oenone starts to speak, she simply reiterates what we already know about the landscape, the silent grasshopper, the noonday quiet, the resting lizard, everything droops or sleeps. At this stage, she is determined to build a monument to her sorrow, to build up her sorrow with her song 'as yonder walls / Rose slowly to a music slowly breathed' (lines 39–40). Troy, or Ilion, supposedly rose like a mist as the god Apollo sang his strange song. Appropriately for the daughter of a river god, Oenone is constantly associated with mists and vapours; like them she is a part of the soft and delicate beauty of the valley. But this scene soon changes.

Chaos accompanies the arrival of the goddesses: 'the crocus brake like fire' (line 94), 'a wind arose' (line 96), and even the ivy and vines begin to run 'riot' (line 99). The scene of the judgement of Paris, it has been said, is actually less a scene of judgement than a scene of temptation. Certainly, Paris is not so much judging who is the fairest as considering the advantages of the various bribes offered. But what is being said about his choice? Traditionally, critics have supported Oenone's spontaneous response that Paris should have awarded the prize to Pallas. In this reading, Herè offers power, almost despotic power perhaps: 'ample rule / Unquestion'd' (lines 109–10). Pallas offers him power over himself: 'Self-reverence, self-knowledge, self-control' (line 142). At this point the language of the poem changes; generally luxuriant and full of concrete descriptive phrases, it now becomes abstract and rather stiff, an appropriate adjustment if Pallas is seen as embodying that which is morally right. But what about Aphrodite, who sidles up so seductively? If we focus upon Aphrodite herself, then perhaps we can claim that Paris is most tempted by pleasure, by sensual delights, and that for this he should be condemned. Drawing back her hair to display her body, she moves closer to Paris and, with a 'subtle smile' (line 180) makes her offer: 'I promise thee / The fairest and most loving wife in Greece' (line 183). Why does she then immediately laugh? Perhaps she is simply all too aware of the weakness of men, but perhaps she also foresees the consequences, the destruction of Troy. Given that Aphrodite fails to mention she is thinking of someone else's wife, however, it is quite conceivable that Paris is tempted less by sensual delights than by the promise of domestic happiness. In this way, we could believe that Paris may be making the right choice. This whole scene makes the notion of choice problematic: how can we know what we are actually choosing? How can we know what the consequences will be?

Once her narrative is finished, Oenone's lament takes a new turn with 'Yet, mother Ida' (line 191). Now she is questioning, more self-assertive. She still wishes that the past could return, and she could again be with Paris and he still be her 'mountain shepherd' (line 198). But now a complete break with the past is suggested. The destruction of her valley, the cutting down of the pines by the Trojans, demonstrates that the distinction between the peaceful valley and the doomed city, first undermined by the arrival of the goddesses, has completely broken down. There is another change when Oenone wishes she could meet 'The Abominable' (line 220), that is, the goddess of discord or strife who caused all these troubles. Oenone is now roused to anger herself. Following this, however, she relapses into nostalgia and begins to wish for death; the **anaphoric** lines of the stanza and the numerous examples of balance and repetition emphasise a desire for all to end, her desire for death. Her tearful memories now become replaced by 'fiery thoughts' (line 242), and her song is full of apocalyptic suggestions. Much of Oenone's lament has been marked by her desire to resist the progress of time, to erect monuments to the past, and this has been formally conveyed by the use of repetition, including the refrain. Now, however, this is replaced by a sense of urgency and movement. More oppositions break down in the final stanza as

Oenone determines to leave her valley and to go down to Troy. Oenone has until now appeared focused upon the past, while Cassandra, as prophetess, focuses upon the future; this distinction also breaks down, and Oenone becomes a kind of prophetess herself, merging with Cassandra. As Cassandra has said 'A fire dances before her' (line 260), so Oenone ends with a similar vision, using language which anticipates both the burning of Troy and her own immolation on Paris's funeral pyre: 'wheresoe'er I am by night and day, / All earth and air seem only burning fire' (lines 263–4).

Ida the mountain on the south of the Troas, setting of the Judgement of Paris

Ionian hills Ionia is an ancient region of Asia Minor, including the Aegean islands, colonised by the Greeks in around 1100 BC

Gargarus the highest point of Mount Ida

Troas the region surrounding Troy

Ilion the Greek name for ancient Troy

Simois one of two rivers on the plain of Troy

Hesperian the Hesperides are the three sisters who guarded the golden apples; the garden where they grew is often referred to as the Garden of the Hesperides

ambrosially ambrosia is the food of the gods; more generally anything delicious

Oread mountain nymph

Peleus it was because Eris, the goddess of discord, was uninvited to the wedding feast of Peleus and Thetis that she cast down the apple

Iris goddess of the rainbow and the messenger of the gods

Herè or Hera, the wife of Zeus, the supreme god of Greek mythology

Pallas Pallas Athene was the patron goddess of Athens and the goddess of wisdom

Aphrodite the goddess of love

amaracus an archaic word for marjoram

peacock sacred to Hera

champaign a made-up archaic word for countryside

Sequel of guerdon addition of reward

Paphian Paphos was a city of Cyprus where Venus was worshipped

pard a leopard or panther

cut away my tallest pines in Ovid's *Amores*, his Oenone complains that the pines have been cut down to make boats for the abduction of Helen

The Abominable a reference to Eris, goddess of discord

the Greek woman Helen, wife of Menelaus, who is given to/abducted by Paris

Cassandra a prophetess; she refused the advances of Apollo and he cursed her so no-one would believe her predictions, although they were always correct

THE LOTOS-EATERS (1832; REV. 1842)

Ulysses's mariners, after eating the lotos or lotus fruit, determine to stay in the Land of the Lotos-Eaters. They sing of their peaceful present existence and express their horror of the hateful world of action

The source for this poem is Homer's *Odyssey*, Book 9, lines 82–104. Ulysses (Odysseus) and his mariners are on their way home to Ithaca after the ten years of war against Troy. The first five stanzas describe Ulysses and his mariners reaching the Land of the Lotos-eaters, a drowsy, languid world where everything moves slowly, where everything 'always seem'd the same' (line 24). The Lotos-eaters appear and offer the enchanted fruit to the weary mariners. They eat the lotus fruit, and enter into a dreamy state in which they sit on the sand and sing, having lost all desire to leave.

This narrative is succeeded by the Choric Song of the drugged mariners. These stanzas alternate between their expressions of delight in the life of ease on the island and their rejection of the past life of strife and action. They sing of the soft sweet music of the island (I). They question why they should be weary and distressed and forced to toil rather than listen to the inner spirit which encourages passivity and calm (II). Considering the natural world, they note how all other things are content and happy simply to live out their natural cycle (III). They reject labour and action, asking to be left alone, to be allowed to rest, to achieve the natural end of death or at least 'dreamful ease' (IV). The notion of dreamful ease which has become their reality is then expanded upon as they consider the sweetness of dreaming, of giving up to 'mild-minded melancholy' and focusing on their memories (V). A rationalisation of their passivity follows as they consider how, while their memories of the past may be sweet, all will now have changed at home: their families will have forgotten them, their lands will have been seized by others (VI). It is much more preferable to stay in the Land of the Lotos-eaters with its many sensual delights (VII). The lotus grows everywhere on the island; they will remain here, living the easeful life of the gods, ignoring the suffering of the outside world (VIII).

This is one of many of Tennyson's poems which deals with the conflict between social responsibility and aesthetic detachment (other poems which could be considered in this context are 'The Palace of Art' and 'The Lady of Shalott'). Structurally, the poem is divided into two main parts: the initial narrative and the Choric Song. The initial narrative consists of a series of five **Spenserian stanzas**, and Tennyson exploits the opportunities offered by such a highly regulated form in two main ways. First, because Spenserian stanzas are so uniform, any deviation from the standard form assumes intense impact. The substitution of **trochee** for **iamb** in the initial foot, therefore, lends particular weight to Ulysses's initial exhortation; the stark, energetic and forceful 'Courage' (line 1) can be said to resound and contrast with the dreamy harmony that follows. This emphatic word becomes representative of an attitude to life, the need to act, to take on responsibilities, that is present by implication throughout the poem, and forms the attitude to life against which that of the Lotos-eaters can be judged. Their following Choric Song can be read as an answer to Ulysses's implicit demands. Secondly, the order, calm and unity of the Spenserian stanza formally imitates the blissful harmony of which the mariners sing, and Tennyson achieves the extraordinary sensuousness associated with Spenser. The mariners wish to renounce the world of strife and social responsibility and commit themselves to a life of withdrawal in a changeless, languid, calm world where they wearily drift in dreamy meditation.

While the introduction of the poem might be expected to be quite different from the Choric Song which follows, in fact, formal similarities mean that the overall feeling of the two parts is much the same. The dreamy movement of the lines of the Choric

Song suggests as much languor as the Spenserian stanzas. The odd-numbered stanzas of the Choric Song emphasise the enervating effects of the lotus and celebrate the cessation of activity; here there is a sense of peace and harmony. In the strikingly **onomatopoeic** opening stanza, for example, the music that is described is formally suggested by the euphonic effects of the language. The stanza is dominated by long vowel sounds, particularly 'ay' ('Than tired eyelids upon tired eyes' line 51) and 'ee' (sweet / sleep / creep / weep); Tennyson even uses 'gentlier' (line 50) rather than 'gentler' to emphasise this effect. The soft **sibilance** suggests that the mariners are just about to stop singing and drift into sleep. In the final three lines, the use of **anaphora** conveys both pleasure and weariness; perhaps even singing is beginning to be just too much; the sense of languid effort is further stressed by the way in which one extra foot is added to the metre of each line. The even-numbered stanzas, however, focus upon the world they have left behind and offer arguments as to why they should not return; here, appropriately reflecting their dislike of that world, there is more of a sense of agitation and discord. This agitation can also be seen as a reaction to being disturbed out of their desired slumber. In stanza IV, for example, harder sounds dominate – mainly **plosives** or **stops** (p, b, t, d, k, g). When juxtaposed these sounds become obstacles to flow. Agitation is also suggested by the **caesuras** and shorter, choppy phrases. The eleven lines of stanza I contain only ten pauses and allow for flow; the fifteen lines of stanza IV have twenty-three pauses and are angrier, more abrupt. 'Let us alone' is their constant refrain, a sign of their irritation at someone trying to disturb their luxurious slumber (see Critical Approaches, on Sound Patterning).

Their new home is a luxuriant but isolated valley, bordered on one side by the hostile sea and on the other by the mountains. There is a sense that time here has stopped; it is a land 'In which it seemèd always afternoon' (line 4). A sense of quiescence pervades all. Even the stream 'Along the cliff to fall and pause and fall did seem' (line 9). They listen to the sweet music of the wind and streams, and wish to 'hear and see the far-off sparkling brine', a wish immediately corrected to 'Only to hear were sweet' (lines 143–4): they do not want to return back to the sea. The life the Lotos-eaters desire is a life of withdrawal in a world where nothing will change. Interestingly, while they appeal to the vegetative life of nature and to the careless life of the gods, they offer no human precedent as justification for their desire for constant ease. It could be said that what the mariners ultimately desire is not to be human, to be dead. Death is, after all, the total end of all action.

Why do you think there is so much repetition in this poem? It is used functionally throughout. Both the opening stanzas and the Choric Song of the men who have rejected strife, action and change for harmony, passivity and stasis are heavily reliant upon anaphora and other correspondences of word and phrase, and by such effects as **alliteration** and **assonance**. The repetition of both sound and word is used in a variety of ways. Sometimes it echoes the tiredness of the mariners to whom 'Most weary seem'd the sea, weary the oar, / Weary the wandering fields of barren foam' (lines 41–2). It can suggest their absolute contentment in this world where 'The flower ripens in its place, / Ripens and fades, and falls, and hath no toil, / Fast-rooted in the fruitful soil' (lines 81–3). However, repetition can also emphasise their irritation at being disturbed or their agitation at the thought of having to return to the old world, as when, in stanza II of the Choric Song, they constantly repeat variations on the phrase 'Why should we toil'.

A frequently repeated word in this poem is 'seemed'. Do you think this might be significant? It 'seems' as if it is always afternoon, it 'seems' as though the falling stream pauses, and things always 'seem' the same. What the word emphasises is perception, the perception of the mariners or Lotos-eaters, and what it suggests is that their perceptions are illusions. Would this also indicate their views are suspect? This is a life lived purely in the mind; there is a complete loss of real communication, a distancing of the outer life: subjectivity becomes all. The even-numbered stanzas, especially those in which the mariners recall the past, continually imply other norms of behaviour by which we might judge their desire for a disengagement from life. In stanza VI of the Choric Song, for example, they quite warmly recall their past lives, their homes, families, and children, but argue that it would be impossible to take up these lives again where they left off: 'all hath suffer'd change' (line 116), they claim, and the use of the word 'suffer' in connection with change is telling. They believe they would no longer be welcome, but the references to household hearths, princes trying to take over their property, and the Trojan war inevitably remind us of the story of Ulysses's wife, Penelope, who remained true and faithful, cleverly warding off other suitors in anticipation of her husband's return. There is, then, a world of fidelity and duty; there is another and more ethical way of living.

In the final stanza, the mariners draw a connection between their own lives and those of the gods. Do you think the predominance of **anapests** rhyming in **tercets** conveys more of a sense of energy and vigour than the previous lines? The mariners are now determined to stay, and their new decisiveness is indicated by the change from 'shall' to 'will': 'we will not wander more' (line 173). It is in this stanza that they appear least sympathetic. They intend to be 'careless of mankind' (line 155), to be like the gods, smiling as they watch the destruction below, the 'wasted lands / Blight and famine, plague and earthquake' (lines 159–60). Indeed, the gods see such human affairs only as forming part of an aesthetic spectacle; they find music in this 'doleful song' (line 162). Ultimately, where do you think the poem places itself with respect to the conflict between social responsibility and aesthetic detachment? The last stanza seems to indicate we should criticise the mariners and judge them guilty of evading their duty. On the other hand, the sensuous detail used to describe the life of the Lotos-eaters does convey its attraction.

Courage! he said the voice of Ulysses
lawn finely woven linen
galingale plant with aromatic roots
amaranth a flower which retains to the end its deep blood-red colour and gave rise to the legend of an immortal unfading flower
moly according to Homer, the mythical herb given to Ulysses as an antidote against the sorceries of the witch Circe

acanthus the leaf form of the *acanthus mollis* was often used to decorate Greek columns

nectar in Greek mythology, the drink of the gods

Elysian in Greek mythology, Elysium was the abode of the blessed after death; Elysian means happy or delightful

asphodel a plant of the lily family, associated with death and the underworld in Greek mythology

THE EPIC (MORTE D'ARTHUR) (1842)

A poet reads his epic about the dying king Arthur and the return of the sword Excalibur to the lady of the lake

The opening frame of 'The Epic' sets up a gathering of friends on Christmas Eve: a poet, a parson, a narrator, and their host, Francis. The poet, Everard Hall, has written a twelve-part **epic** on King Arthur. Considering such work to be anachronistic, he had decided to burn it. Francis, however, has saved the eleventh book of this Arthuriad from the fire, and Everard is persuaded to read it aloud to his friends. This is the 'Morte d'Arthur', a poem which Tennyson eventually revised and incorporated into 'The Passing of Arthur' (1870), the last of his *Idylls of the King*. The 'Morte d'Arthur' focuses primarily on the interaction between the dying Arthur and Bedivere, his last knight. Arthur tells Bedivere to throw the sword Excalibur into the lake and then to return and report what he sees. Bedivere tries three times to cast the sword away. The first time he is dazzled by the beauty of the sword and hides it; the second time he persuades himself that the sword must be retained to prove the story of Arthur. Finally, shamed by Arthur, Bedivere succeeds in throwing the sword into the lake. An arm appears from the lake and takes the sword. Bedivere then carries the dying Arthur to the side of the lake where he is received by three queens in a barge. In the closing frame of 'The Epic', the narrator suggests 'Perhaps some modern touches here and there / Redeem'd it from the charge of nothingness' (lines 278–9). That night the narrator dreams of sailing with Arthur, now like 'a modern gentleman' (line 294), and of the welcome Arthur is given, as he represents the return of 'all good things' (line 300) and the end of war.

What function do you think the opening frame serves in this poem? When the parson bemoans the loss of religious faith, Frances claps his hand on Hall's shoulder and says 'I hold by him'. Part of the point of the opening frame is, then, to suggest that in a world where there is 'no anchor, none, / To hold by' (lines 20–1), poetry can fill the place left void by the decline of religious faith (see Critical Approaches, on Science and Religion, and Historical & Literary Background). The notion of necessary progression indicated by this claim anticipates what Bedivere will discover in the following tale. There is no point in clinging to the old (as the parson and Bedivere want to do); one must move towards accepting the new order, a new set of values and beliefs. The contrast between old and new is also indicated by the distinction in the style and language of the frame and the tale itself: the more natural language of the former is offset by the formal, archaic and ritualistic language of the latter. Of course, the tale itself does in a sense cling to the old, and this frame narrative also raises the question of how relevant and acceptable medieval legend might be to a contemporary audience. Hall burned his twelve-book epic, he tells his friends, out of a feeling that there is little use in reworking the stories of Arthur:

'Why take the style of those heroic times?
For nature brings not back the Mastodon,
Nor we those times; and why should any man
Remodel models?' (lines 35–8)

Do you think this question is answered by the poem itself? The 'Morte d'Arthur', like the later *Idylls of the King* into which it becomes incorporated, can be said to use the past as a way of discussing contemporary issues and problems while maintaining an aesthetic distance. This was an age when faith was being submitted to many tests by scientific discoveries, and the epic demonstrates, through the failure of the Round Table, what happens when people lose faith in their ideals. At the same time, it urges the need for continuing faith, and more optimistically suggests that Bedivere will take these ideals into the new age. Most epics are concerned with the transmission of stories and with the transmission of the values of a culture. Herbert Tucker, in

Tennyson and the Doom of Romanticism, has demonstrated that one of the key motifs in this poem is that of transmission. But as Tucker demonstrates, Tennyson's 'Morte d'Arthur' is not so much concerned to transmit a story, a culture, as it is concerned with exploring the actual *process* of transmission itself. The poem suggests culture is not something fixed to be passed on through stories: culture is the process of change and transmission. What do you think the three main stages of transmission might be in this poem? The first is surely the need for Bedivere to transfer the sword back to the lady of the lake; the second is for Bedivere to take Arthur down to the lake; the third is for the three Queens to take Arthur away in their barge.

Why do you think Tennyson begins 'So all day long …' (line 52) as though we had just read the previous part of the story? He is drawing upon an epic tradition, starting **in medias res**. There are other epic conventions in the 'Morte d'Arthur', including the use of the **epic simile** and the **epithet**; the most notable epithet is the somewhat **ironic** 'bold Sir Bedivere'. Do you think the descriptions of the setting are functional in this tale? It is set in the middle of winter on a 'dark strait of barren land' (line 10). This is a significant change from Malory, who sets the last battle in the summer. It is 'a place of tombs' (line 46), 'pointed rock' (line 50), and 'bare black cliffs' (line 188). The setting appropriately suggests death and desolation.

The question of storytelling and transmission is stressed from the start. Arthur tells Bedivere to throw into the lake the sword Excalibur; Excalibur, he believes, will be an essential part of the story and its origins known 'wheresoever I am sung or told / In aftertime' (line 34). When Bedivere first tries to throw away the sword, he fails because he is dazzled by its beauty; he sees it as a valuable aesthetic object. Arthur is angered not so much because he fails to throw the sword as because he lies: 'Thou hast betrayed thy nature and thy name' (line 73); he has not acted as befits a noble knight and therefore has undermined all the ideals represented by the Round Table. The second time Bedivere fails because he convinces himself the king 'knows not what he does' (line 97) and so should not be obeyed; he now sees the sword as a sign, something that should be kept as a 'record' or 'relic' of Arthur in order that the story should not be forgotten. In valuing the sword as precious object or meaningful sign, however, he disobeys the king, and, in so doing, betrays the underlying principles of which the sword is simply the physical sign. When Bedivere finally succeeds in throwing the sword into the lake, the description suggests the passing of the whole history of Arthur into myth and story-telling as it is received by the 'arm/ Clothed in white samite, mystic, wonderful' (lines 158–9). Significantly, this is also the moment when Tennyson first draws upon one of the main features of traditional epic: the epic simile. Flashing and whirling like the northern lights, the 'great brand', he notes 'Shot like a streamer of the northern morn, / Seen where the moving isles of winter shock / By night, with noises of the northern sea' (lines 139–41).

In the last part of the poem, Tucker observes, the epic similes become more frequent, and this is surely significant for a poem concerned with the process of transmission, with the transmission of history into myth or story. We can see Arthur becoming epic material as the poem progresses. Once Bedivere achieves his goal, Arthur, now ready for the next stage, half-rises slowly, reclining on his arm, 'And looking wistfully with wide blue eyes / As in a picture' (lines 169–70). Action is momentarily replaced by this frozen pictorial moment, but the narrative is then pushed onwards as the second stage in the process of transmission begins.

Assonance and **alliteration** are used to effect throughout this poem, and the language formally reproduces the feelings described. As Bedivere carries Arthur to the lake, his difficult progress is aptly suggested by the language:

Dry clash'd his harness in the icy caves
And barren chasms, and all to left and right
The bare black cliff clang'd round him, as he based
His feet on juts of slippery crag that rang
Sharp-smitten with the dint of armèd heels – (lines 186–90)

The words here, as often in the *Morte d'Arthur*, are mainly monosyllabic; the diction is concrete, measured and precise; the alliterative effects of such groupings as clash'd – chasms – cliff – clanged – crag are suggestive of harshness and the difficulties Bedivere encounters. The description is not only visual but aural; we hear the clash of the armour among the echoing cliffs and the ringing of his heels on the crags. There is a repeated use of **enjambment**, which suggests Bedivere's determined progression onwards. When he finally arrives at their destination, the successful conclusion of his struggle is indicated as the scene is transformed into something beautiful and harmonious: 'And on a sudden, lo! the level lake, / And the long glories of the winter moon' (lines 191–2). Bedivere and Arthur have moved through a harsh physical landscape to arrive, as the appearance of the dusky barge with its 'decks dense with stately forms … like a dream' suggests, in the world of myth. Arthur will now go through the final process of being restored to his legendary home.

For the first time grief is allowed release, given full play. The three Queens who will escort Arthur are standing on the barge,

> … and from them rose
> A cry that shiver'd to the tingling stars,
> And, as it were one voice, an agony
> Of lamentation, like a wind, that shrills
> All night in a waste land, where no one comes,
> Or hath come, since the making of the world. (lines 198–203)

It is difficult to imagine how the agony of grief could be more effectively conveyed. The 'tingling' stars themselves seem to react to the shrill, piercing cry. As the epic simile suggests, this is indeed now a wasteland, a world of death. The desolation of the landscape indicates not only the death of an old order, the death of Arthur and the dissolution of the Round Table, but also the desolation of Sir Bedivere who still cannot relinquish this order: 'Ah! my Lord Arthur, whither shall I go?' he cries, 'For now I see the true old times are dead' (lines 227–9); he, the last of Arthur's knights, must 'go forth companionless' (line 236). Bedivere once again laments the loss of the visual, physical sign, the Round Table which 'was an image of the mighty world' (line 235). He equates the time of Arthur and the Round Table with the birth of Christianity, with the wise men guided by the light of the star to the child in Bethlehem. Now, he sees nothing ahead but darkness. Arthur's response at first seems to offer little comfort:

> The old order changeth, yielding place to new,
> And God fulfils Himself in many ways,
> Lest one good custom should corrupt the world.
> Comfort thyself: what comfort is in me? (lines 240–243)

While this may suggest a kind of mindless change without conscious effort or reason, Arthur in fact then goes on to suggest how a new order can be created, and that this is now up to Bedivere. He may go alone into a dark new world, but he will take with him the story, and can transmit the values to which the best of the others, in this new world, will respond. The physical Arthur may be gone, but the values he represents can have an enduring influence, and, as Tucker observes, 'the medium of this succession is language, in its work of representing what is absent' (page 342). 'Pray for my soul', Arthur instructs Bedivere, 'More things are wrought by prayer / Than this world dreams of. Wherefore, let thy voice / Rise like a fountain for me night and day' (lines 247–9). Bedivere is left, 'Revolving many memories' (line 270), as the barge sails not into the sunset, with its associations with endings but into the sunrise, suggestive of new beginnings; the story is now for him to tell. Appropriately, then, when Tennyson incorporates the 'Morte d'Arthur' into the *Idylls of the King* under the title 'The Passing of Arthur', he begins by demonstrating how Bedivere does indeed become part of the new process of transmission by describing the idyll as:

> That story which the bold Sir Bedivere,
> First made and latest left of all his knights,
> Told, when the man was no more than a voice
> In the white winter of his age, to those
> With whom he dwelt, new faces, other minds (lines 1–5)

forfeits a game in which players have to give up an object or perform an action if they make mistakes

schism division of a group into factions, here, specifically the Church

Mastodon extinct mammal

Lyonnesse the country of legend that lies between Cornwall and the Scilly Islands

chancel part of a church containing the altar

Camelot the legendary place where Arthur held his court

brand sword

Excalibur the sword which Arthur was given by the lady of the lake

samite a heavy silk fabric

lief life: as thou art life and dear to me

mere lake

casque helmet

greaves and cuisses armour for shin and thigh

lists field of combat at a tournament

Avilion or Avalon, the Island of the Blessed

ULYSSES (1842)

An aging Ulysses expresses his dissatisfaction with his life at home on Ithaca, and his desire for one last adventure before he dies

According to myth, Ulysses (Odysseus) was one of the Greek kings who went to war with Troy after the abduction of Helen. The *Iliad* tells the story of this war, while the *Odyssey* focuses upon the ten-year wanderings and eventual return of Ulysses to Ithaca. One of Tennyson's sources is the eleventh book of the *Odyssey*, in which it is foretold that Ulysses, after his return, will set off on another voyage. Another source is Dante's *Inferno* (Canto xxvi, lines 90–142), where Ulysses is in hell for the sin of fraud and guile; he tells the story of his death at sea on a final voyage. In Tennyson's **dramatic monologue**, Ulysses, after having been home for some time, expresses his dissatisfaction with his life of inaction. Idle, he is confined to Ithaca with his now ancient wife Penelope and his 'savage' (line 4) people. His love of life is expressed in the second stanza, where he also notes how he achieved his great name. There is no end to experience, he believes, and no end to his desire for new experience and for knowledge. He has little time left to live and he does not want simply to store and hoard what is left or to accept limits on possibility. In the next stanza he introduces his son Telemachus, temperamentally more suited to rule and civilise the people than Ulysses himself. In the concluding stanza, Ulysses turns to his mariners, recalling what they have done together; they may be old, he says, but something noble may yet be done. They will sail into the unknown, perhaps to die, perhaps to reach the Happy Isles where they will meet the great hero Achilles again. They may not be the men they were, but they still possess their heroic hearts and will not give up; they remain 'strong in will / To strive, to seek, to find, and not to yield' (line 70).

> 'Ulysses' offers an excellent demonstration of Tennyson's ability to control deftly the form of **blank verse**. Blank verse is particularly useful in dramatic monologues because of its relative closeness to spoken English. What specific techniques does Tennyson use to convey the sense of a person speaking in this dramatic monologue? Does the tone of the speaker shift in each section? Generally, we can say that the unrhymed lines of **iambic pentameter** are manipulated to create a wide variety of tones. This is achieved through the use of the **caesura** and **enjambment**, through the addition of variation from the iambic norm, often with the use of an initial **trochee**, and through the skilful control of language.
>
> In a dramatic monologue, the speaker generally addresses an auditor. Who do you think Ulysses is addressing in this poem? Does the auditor appear to change? It is difficult to say whom he is addressing in the first section, perhaps at this stage no-one. Certainly, Ulysses is not likely to be addressing his poor wife or his maligned people. What insights do these first five lines give us into Ulysses's character? From the snarling scornfulness of the opening lines, we become quickly aware that Ulysses is dissatisfied, frustrated. Ithaca and its people are associated with negative qualities; in this world one is 'idle', 'still', 'barren' and 'savage' (lines 1–4). There is also a preponderance of words that suggest measurement or limitation, and Ulysses himself repeatedly resists any attempt by the world or even by death to impose limits upon the self. On the other hand, he speaks of there being little

'profit' (line 1) to him in carrying out the responsibilities of kingship. At this stage he appears more concerned with self-interest and gain than in civilising and helping his people. He resents being 'Match'd' (line 3) with an aging wife, and the initial replacement of the iambic norm by a trochee here reinforces a sense of contempt. (Ulysses's wife, Penelope, it might be worth remembering, had waited twenty years for her husband to return, putting off her many other suitors and remaining faithful to him always.) There is a hardness to the language in this opening section, partly the effect of insistent and grating monosyllables in such lines as 'That hoard, and sleep, and feed, and know not me' (line 5). Ulysses describes his people in animalistic, or perhaps mechanistic, terms. The harshness is further stressed by the extremely heavy and regular **iambs**, the regularity made more pronounced by the pauses caused by the commas. Do you think it is significant that these bitter and frustrated lines end with the emphatic 'me' (line 5)? There is a clear sense of pride, even egocentricity here. Ulysses wants to define himself, not to be defined by his social context, his responsibilities as husband and ruler. He desires something more than this static world has to offer, to consume something more than the food upon which his people feed.

What he desires to consume, as he explains in the second section, is experience itself: to 'drink / Life to the lees' (lines 6–7) and to roam with 'a hungry heart' (line 12). The **metaphorical** use of the language of consumption, through its connection and contrast with the habits of the 'savage' people who 'hoard, and sleep, and feed', draws attention to the differences between these people and the aging speaker and emphasises his more heroic qualities. As Ulysses remembers his past adventures, the tone changes. The hard contempt is replaced by something flowing, lyrical and **rhetorical**. What contributes to this effect? The lines are frequently enjambed, echoing Ulysses's own claim that it is dull 'to pause, to make an end' (line 22). There is the use of repetition, which suggests harmony, and this, along with the use of such lists as 'manner, climates, councils, governments' (line 14), builds up the excitement Ulysses experiences as, in memory, he is released from the confines of

Ithaca to a more expansive active world. Again, there is the suggestion of egocentricity in such lines as 'I am become a name' (line 11) and 'I am a part of all that I have met' (line 18), but Ulysses now appears a much more impressive figure. The insatiable nature of desire is indicated by the **metaphor** of experience as an arch; as the seeker after experience travels closer, the margin fades further away; it will never be reached.

When Ulysses turns to his son, there is an implied gesture along with the opening line: 'This is my son, mine own Telemachus'. This is perhaps when Ulysses begins to address his people. Some critics have seen this passage as suggestive of Ulysses's abandonment of his responsibilities and a dismissive attitude towards Telemachus's talents. Others consider this much more complimentary, showing Ulysses's esteem for his son's abilities in a sphere to which he is intelligent enough to recognise he is himself unsuited. What changes do you see in the language now? The language could be said to exemplify all the qualities of prudence and decorum he is praising in his son. The rhythms are much more subdued and controlled; the diction more abstract, flatter, even rather drab and certainly much less imagistic; the tone is calm and reserved, showing none of the enthusiasm of the previous section. We might be suspicious of Ulysses's tendency to define his son's virtues by negation: 'Most blameless is he' and 'decent not to fail' (lines 39–40). Overall, however, Ulysses presents himself far more moderately here. Even his description of his people is modified from 'savage' to 'rugged' (line 37) – a diplomatic decision since he appears to be addressing them. But this reconstruction of his people alerts us to the fact that what Ulysses says here for public consumption suggests quite a different attitude towards kingship and towards his people than his private musings have implied.

In the final section Ulysses addresses his mariners. While previously he has rejected community, now he attempts to construct one, one that will, however, serve his particular purposes. He appeals to them with the idea of work, of 'toil' or 'some work of noble note' (lines 50–2). What does Ulysses seek; what do you think his goals, his aims, are? Perhaps what he desires is too unfocused to answer this question. He wants to have something more, some 'newer world' (line 57), to have 'something ere the end' (line 51), but what this something is remains vague; it seems as though all he desires is an endless succession of new and challenging experiences. Tennyson himself reflected something of this vagueness when he said this poem revealed his 'feeling about the need of going forward and braving the struggle of life' (Hallam Tennyson, *Alfred Lord Tennyson: A Memoir*, 1897, vol.1, p. 196). Does this accord with your own feelings about the poem? For many readers, the monologue conveys as much a sense of retreat as a sense of going forward. There is, for example, the fact that one thing Ulysses hopes for is to join Achilles on the Happy Isles, where the virtuous dead dwell after death; that is surely an expression, even if a sublimated expression, of a death wish. Indeed death, some critics have suggested, is implicit throughout the poem, in the darkness of the seas and the seductive slowness of the rhythms. But Ulysses does not give in to death; he challenges it. Do you think this results in a certain tension in the poem? A good example of possible tension comes when Ulysses addresses his men: 'The lights begin to twinkle from the rocks: / The long day wanes: the slow moon climbs: the deep / Moans round with many voices' (lines 55–7). The slow movement here, with the emphatic **caesuras**, the skilful use of **assonance**, the lingering on long vowel sounds, may give Ulysses dignity and power, but they are also quite hypnotic, perhaps suggesting a desire for oblivion. Ultimately, perhaps, we could say that the poem does indeed express a desire for retreat, for death, but that this is challenged at the same time as it is expressed. Ulysses heroically resists the seduction to yield, asserting his will, urging on his men to remain 'strong in will / To strive, to seek, to find, and not to yield' (lines 69–70).

Hyades in Greek myth, seven nymphs who were placed among the stars; the rising of these stars was associated with the coming of storms
Troy the fortress city attacked by the Greeks when the Trojan prince Paris abducted Helen, wife of the Greek king Menelaus
household gods those thought to preside over dwellings and domestic concerns in the ancient world

Happy Isles where the virtuous dead dwell; the isles of the blessed
Achilles hero of the *Iliad*

BREAK, BREAK, BREAK (1842)

An expression of grief caused by loss

The speaker observes the sea breaking on the rocks. He wishes he could give voice to the anguish he feels. Life goes on around him unchanged: the fisherman's boy shouts at play with his sister, the sailor sings in his boat, and the ships continue onwards. However, the thought of their imminent disappearance, as they vanish over the horizon, makes him turn back to his own sorrow and think of the vanished hand he wants to touch and the now silenced voice he wants to hear. The sounds of the sea go on, and he accepts that what is finished can never return.

One of Tennyson's simplest and most beautiful lyrics, 'Break, break, break' manages to express deep grief and an anguished sense of loss without ever descending into overstatement or the maudlin. The language of the poem is restrained and simple, and the descriptions are of ordinary, everyday things. The opening line of the first and final stanzas, 'Break, break, break', consists of three heavily stressed syllables, and echoes the heaviness of the speaker's heart. In the first stanza, the 'cold gray stones' (line 2) he observes convey a sense of nature's indifference to human loss. The speaker wants to give voice to the 'thoughts that arise in me' (line 4), and while his tongue seems incapable of uttering these thoughts, the lyric itself effectively succeeds in suggesting them. The children at play, the sailor and the ship, all are going on with life and are quite unaware of his sorrow. In the second stanza, the exclamation 'O' and the actual exclamation marks convey happiness and delight. These cries of delight, however, serve only to remind him of a now silenced voice. How different is the effect of the 'O' and the exclamation mark when he declares 'But O for the touch of a vanish'd hand, / And the sound of a voice that is still!' (lines 11–12)? Here we have deep sorrow and frustrated desire. The second line in this stanza is one of two four-foot lines in a poem for which the norm is three-foot lines. The other four-foot line is 'But the tender grace of a day that is dead' (line 15). What do you think the effect is of the variation?

The rushing movement of the **anapests** certainly offers a contrast to the powerful slow beats of 'Break, break, break'. Do you think Tennyson's use of **synecdoche** in this lyric is functional? Why does he say he wishes his *tongue* could utter the thoughts and not that he wishes *he* could utter the thoughts? This might not seem of much significance if it were not that the lost individual is also synecdochally referred to as a 'vanish'd hand' (line 11) and the 'sound of a voice' (line 12). Why does Tennyson not just refer to the dead person? Partly this use of synecdoche places more emphasis on the senses themselves and by implication more on the loss on physical and aural connection; it is not just that he misses someone, he misses specifically the communication with that person. In the final stanza, do you think there is more of a sense of acceptance? The last two lines of this stanza are certainly calmer and softer than the last two lines of the first stanza, where 'And I would that' (line 3) evokes a continuing anguish rather than acceptance. In the final stanza, the poem formally circles back to the start through repetition of 'Break, break, break', but while the sea continues to provide an image of an endless natural cycle, a constant return, the speaker himself accepts nothing can bring back, restore, what he has lost, that 'Tender grace of a day that is dead / Will never come back to me' (lines 15–16). Of course, we could say that it has in fact come back, in the very process of remembering, but the idea of the **paradoxical** presence of what is absent is more clearly explored in the lyric 'Tears, Idle Tears' (see Themes).

THE PRINCESS: A MEDLEY (1847)·

> **Seven friends decide to improvise a tale. This becomes the story of Princess Ida, who has founded a university for women, and the Prince to whom she had been betrothed in childhood and whom she has rejected**

This tale in 3,309 lines of **blank verse** is interspersed with a number of lyrics, also in blank verse, such as 'Tears, idle tears', and with various songs, which were added in 1850. A more detailed discussion of two of these poems will be given below (see also Extended Commentaries). Although they are frequently read out of context, it is much more useful to know the story and situation in which they occur, and so a summary of this follows. The Prologue sets up the scene with seven university friends who decide to improvise a tale in seven parts. It begins with a prince, the narrator, who has been betrothed to the Princess Ida since birth. She announces she will not marry and, believing that women are equal to men although treated like children, she founds a women's university. The Prince and two friends, Cyril and Florian, disguise themselves as women and gain access to the university. Lady Psyche, one of the two main lecturers, recognises Florian as her brother; she asks them how they had missed the inscription over the entrance, 'Let no man enter in on pain of death', but eventually agrees to keep their secret. The three men are invited to join in an academic expedition. At evening they go to their tent, and Cyril's behaviour reveals them to be men. The women flee, and Princess Ida falls in a river only to be saved by the Prince; she is nevertheless still adamant that the men must die. The Prince's father sends an army and the Princess reluctantly lets them go. When the Princess's brother also arrives with an army, a fight appears inevitable. They decide on a tournament with fifty men from each side. The Prince is injured and Ida nurses him as the university is turned into a hospital to cope with all the wounded men. Ida falls in love with the Prince and the tale ends happily with their marriage. In the Conclusion, the seven friends argue over the significance of their story.

'TEARS, IDLE TEARS, I KNOW NOT WHAT THEY MEAN' (1847)

A meditation upon the paradoxical presence of absence

As soon as this lyric, sung by an unnamed girl, is finished, Princess Ida denounces it. Let the past be past, she declares, claiming it is better to focus on the prospects for the future than the delights of the past. Furthermore, she adds, drawing upon the image of Ulysses and the Sirens,

> ... If indeed there haunt
> About the mouldered lodges of the Past
> So sweet a voice and vague, fatal to men,
> Well needs it we should cram our ears with wool
> And so pace by. (IV, lines 44–8)

But the Princess is wrong on two counts. First, as critics have recognised, the poem is not actually thinking about the days that are no more, but thinking about *thinking* about these days (see Themes). Second, the past and the present are not so easily kept apart as she would like to believe. We think of the irrecoverable past, as this poem suggests, and the very thought of thinking about it brings it back to us. A series of **similes** are offered to suggest the nature of inner feelings through descriptions of more concrete events and objects. In the second stanza, the process of remembering makes past days recalled as fresh as the first beam glittering on a sail bringing lost friends up from the underworld, and the sadness of those days to the last beam glittering on that sail as it sinks, 'with all we love' (line 9), below the verge. There is an emphasis here on the liminal state: the friends are either on their way up or sinking back down. Similarly, in the third stanza, the days that are no more are as sad and strange as the sounds of 'half-awaken'd birds / To dying ears' when in the dawn light, the window 'slowly grows a glimmering square' (lines 12–14). Again, there is the emphasis on the in-between state. As Herbert Tucker notes, the '**oxymoronic** balance of approach and recession throughout these stanzas convincingly renders not a specific set of memories but the very experience of remembering' (*Tennyson and the Doom of Romanticism*, Harvard University Press, 1988, p. 364). The final stanza takes us across the threshold into the state of death itself. The line 'Dear as remember'd kisses after death' (line 16) is interestingly ambiguous: it can suggest us remembering the kisses previously given by those now dead; it can also suggest that the actual corpse might find the memory of kisses dear after death. While most of the poem has been written in long, luxuriant phrases, now we are presented with a series of short clauses: 'deep as love, / Deep as first love, and wild with all regret' (lines 18–19), moving the reader along to the final **paradoxical** description of the days that are no more. Why should the days that are no more be **apostrophised** as 'Death in Life'? The phrase summarises everything the poem has said about the way what is dead and lost paradoxically remains alive and present within the memory.

> When compared to another poem about loss and absence, 'Break, break, break', this particular poem seems much more impersonal. The speaker may begin by saying 'Tears, idle tears, I know not what

they mean' (line 1), but, after this, the experience of tears is more universalised. Tears rise to 'the' eyes (line 3) and not 'my' eyes. It is 'our friends' (line 7) and what 'we love' (line 9) that form the focus; this is not the expression of a private grief. The two poems also offer an interesting contrast in formal terms. 'Break, break, break' uses the conventional strategy of **end-rhyme** to construct stability and coherence. 'Tears, idle tears' is written in **blank verse** and is therefore unrhymed; the language and formal arrangement of the poem, however, supplies much of the same sense of coherence, stability and order that the presence of rhyme offers. There is the ending of each stanza with the refrain 'the days that are no more'; there is a heavy use of **end-stopped** lines; and there is also the use of **internal rhyme** and **assonance**, in such phrases as 'slowly grows' and other variations on the repetition of sound, such as the **alliterative** effect of 'sad and strange or 'depth of some divine despair'.

'COME DOWN, O MAID, FROM YONDER MOUNTAIN HEIGHT' (1850)

The shepherd begs the maid to leave the icy and alien mountains and come down to the warm human valley

This is the second song Ida reads by the bed of the injured Prince (for a discussion of the first, see Extended Commentaries, Text 1). The poem is in the *carpe diem* tradition. The shepherd pleads with the maid to leave the cold and sterile heights of the hills and come down to the valley. Love can be found only in the warm and human valley; it cannot be found on the icy mountains where eagles yelp. In the valley he, her shepherd, is piping, the children are calling, and every sound is sweet.

The shepherd who sings this lyric sets up a number of striking oppositions between the mountains and the valley. How does Tennyson use differing types of **alliterative** and **assonantal** effects to suggest the contrast between the two worlds? Although the shepherd asserts there is little pleasure in height, in fact, he does recognise the 'splendour of the hills' (line 3). But it is clearly a cold and hard splendour, and this is effectively conveyed through such lines as when the shepherd urges her 'cease / To glide a sunbeam by the blasted Pine, / To sit a star upon the sparkling spire' (lines 4–6). There is the chilly repetition of the 'ay' sound and an emphatic use of **sibilance**. The effect of sibilance here is quite different from its softer effect when combined with the long drawn out 'ee' sound in 'and sweet is every sound, / Sweeter thy voice, but every sound is sweet' (lines 27–28). As the shepherd claims that in the valley all sounds are sweet, so Tennyson's language creates this sweetness of sound. This is particularly notable in the highly **euphonic** final lines, with their striking use of **onomatopoeia**, which describe a far more tamed landscape than is found in the heights:

Myriads of rivulets hurrying thro' the lawn,
The moan of doves in immemorial elms,
And murmuring of innumerable bees' (lines 30–1).

The soft murmuring sound is also anticipated in the shepherd's earlier repetition of the word 'come' as he urges the maid: 'And come, for Love is of the valley, come, / For Love is of the valley, come thou down' (lines 7–8). Such pleasant sounds, associated with the valley, are contrasted with the discordant yelp of the eagle associated with the mountains. Tennyson draws upon all kinds of sensory contrasts in this poem. That which is chilly and hard and silver or white is offset by that which is warm and soft and coloured in vibrant reds and purples. You should be able to find numerous other sets of oppositions in this lyric that characterise the distinction between mountain and valley. One of particular importance is the opposition between isolation and community. In the mountains, the maid's only 'human' companions will be **personified** Death and Morning. But in the valley, her shepherd waits and the children call.

What do you think of the strange **simile** in the description of the high clouds as 'wreaths of dangling water-smoke, / That like a broken purpose waste in air: / So waste not thou; but come' (lines 22–4)? If the context of this lyric is recalled, the simile is particularly apt. Ida has decided to leave her own lofty heights, and has given in to the love of the Prince; her own purpose, then, to reject all men, has been broken.

IN MEMORIAM A.H.H. (1850)

An expression of grief for the death of Arthur Hallam. The poem also engages with the problem of how to retain faith in God in the face of scientific evidence to the contrary

Begun in 1833 after the death of Hallam, *In Memoriam* consists of 131 lyrics of between three and thirty stanzas, rhyming *abba*, and is framed by a Prologue and Epilogue. Critics have often denied that the whole strives for or achieves any particular unity or coherence. T.S. Eliot, for example, considered it to be much like a diary. Tennyson, however, claimed it had a tripartite structure, marked out by the three successive Christmasses (lyrics 28, 78, and 104). While it is impossible to summarise all 131 lyrics, it may be useful to divide the poem into sections as follows.

The opening lyrics of section one (i–viii) offer the most despairing phase of grief. Sorrow causes Tennyson to deny the existence of God and he refuses all hope. He visits Hallam's house, but the whole world seems as bleak as this now silent and empty house. In section two (ix–xx) the mood is calmer. In spirit he accompanies the ship carrying Arthur's remains home. Section three (xxi–vii) includes recollections of Hallam; Tennyson wonders if the years of friendship were as perfect as they now seem, but concludes life was easier when he had his friend. He considers 'it is better to have loved and lost / Than never to have loved at all.' Section four (xxvii–xlix) begins with the Christmas bells, a traditional sign of hope, and there is speculation about the state of life after death. Section five (l–lviii) offers a period of uncertainty and questioning; he wants to trust that good will triumph and that no forms of life will ever be completely destroyed, but feels he is like 'An infant crying for the light'. Nature seems indifferent to both the individual and the species. Section six (lix–lxxi) suggests communication with Hallam is still possible. Hallam appears to him in a series of dreams. Section seven (lxxii–xcviii) begins with the anniversary of Hallam's death; a second Christmas passes. He thinks of Hallam's great talents. There is a turning point when, reading Hallam's letters one night, the 'living soul' is flashed on his and the two are fused, entwined; there is a sense of spiritual oneness. Section eight (xcix–ciii) opens with the anniversary of Hallam's death. The Tennysons are leaving Somersby and scenes dear to both himself and Hallam cause further feelings of regret. The final section (civ–cxxi) shows Tennyson deciding not to brood over sorrow. Geological evidence and his own failure to find God in nature do not destroy his faith that God is love, and that the human race may continue to progress. Hallam is associated with evolving good; he is a noble, superior type of being. In spite of scientific evidence, subjective religious feelings make it possible to retain a belief in God and in an afterlife. More detailed analysis of selected sections is given below (see also Extended Commentaries, Text 2).

OLD YEW, WHICH GRASPEST AT THE STONES (II)

The speaker **apostrophises** the yew tree, an evergreen tree commonly planted in churchyards as it is a **symbol** of immortality. The way the branches of the tree grasp the headstones while the roots entwine themselves around the skull and bones of the dead suggests a human desire, the intense desire of the speaker to touch his dead friend. The second stanza seems to offer the traditional consolation of the seasons which come round again each year. At first the language is harmonious and comforting, referring to the blooming of the first flowers and the birth of the first lambs in the spring. But then there is a change as 'the clock / Beats out the little lives of men' (lines 7–8). The third stanza suggests that this tree is set apart from the rest of nature, remaining the same all year and always fixed upon, grasping and embracing the dead. He envies the hardiness of the tree and determines he too will resist change, and envisions becoming one with the yew tree's devoted but sullen embrace. In 'incorporating' (line 16) himself into the tree – and we might consider whether the word is chosen for its closeness to 'corpse' – the speaker can join in with the embrace of the dead.

CALM IS THE MORN WITHOUT A SOUND (XI)

Sections IX and X have described the speaker's concern about the safe return of Hallam's body in a ship. The speaker now considers his own return to relative calmness and peace as he contemplates the calm landscape. His eye moves gradually over the countryside until it reaches the sea. In the final stanza there is a sudden recognition of what 'dead calm' actually means for Hallam's body, now coming home by sea.

Calm is clearly the central focus of this section, and its centrality is indicated by the repetition of the word, a repetition emphasised by Tennyson's use of **parallelism**. Alan Sinfield has also drawn attention to the fact that this section contains remarkably few transitive verbs, and relates this to the sense of stillness that Tennyson conveys. There may also be the echo of a lullaby in the rhythms and repetition of the lyric. Calm, however, has more than one meaning here. There is the calm of the landscape, the calm despair of the poet, and finally the dead calm of Hallam. The calm which is in the heart of the poet is quite different from the calm in Hallam's heart. The speaker's heart is presented as the seat of emotions, but Hallam's is significantly the organ of life itself. In the final stanza, the human attributes that Hallam should have, the ability to breathe and sleep and move with conscious intent, are transferred on to the sea itself, and we recognise what 'dead calm' means for 'that noble breast / Which heaves but with the heaving deep' (lines 19–20): the heart has stopped, Hallam is dead, and any heaving of the breast is simply an illusion of life created by the sea. When we return to look again at the initial description of the landscape, death seems implicit within this autumn scene from the start. The poem begins with morning sunlight, the spider webs glistening in the morning dew, and ends in moonlight, with the silver sleep of the sea.

BE NEAR ME WHEN MY LIGHT IS LOW (L)

The speaker begins by pleading with his friend to remain near him and comfort him 'when my light is low' (line 1). The **metaphorical** language here is richly suggestive. The speaker's state of mind is associated with the burning down of a candle which may variously indicate depression, the loss of vigour and vitality, and, if light is associated with spiritual belief, with the loss of faith. The image also makes the speaker appear much like a child fearful of the dark. There is, however, an interesting reversal on this conventional image. The language may be associated with fear of ghosts – the blood 'creeps' and the nerves 'prick / And tingle' (lines 2–3) – but in fact the ghost is called upon to appear and offer comfort; it is the absence, not the presence, of the ghost that prompts the fear. The poem then moves away from the personal and physical to consider two more general and abstract images. Time, **personified** as 'a maniac scattering dust' (line 7), appears irrational and destructive, with 'dust' suggesting the possibility of total extinction. Life, equally malevolent, is 'a Fury slinging flame' (line 8). The third stanza then calls upon Hallam to comfort him when his faith has gone – the word used is 'dry' (line 9), looking back to the dust of extinction. Humankind becomes 'the flies of latter spring' (line 10), with their short lives. Finally, the speaker turns to his own moment of death. The **parallelism** of the opening lines of each stanza creates a sense of a building up of intensity to this final moment when Tennyson plays further variations on the image of light. The low burning light of stanza one now becomes the fading away of life itself, leading to the darkness of death and then into the twilight which ultimately gives way to the renewal of light in 'eternal day' (line 16). The section consequently ends on a much more positive note: the idea of simple extinction being replaced with the possibility of spiritual rebirth in another world where his friend may indeed be once again near him.

'SO CAREFUL OF THE TYPE?' BUT NO (LVI)

The previous section offers the hope that while Nature may seem to have little concern for the individual, she does at least preserve the type. This section, marking the climax of despair, challenges even this comforting belief. Individual loss is now put aside and the fear is of the extinction of the whole human race. As if in answer to both the fearful cry of the abandoned infant in section LIV and the speaker's remark that Nature seems at least 'careful of the type' in section LV, there is the shriek of a ferocious mother Nature: 'I care for nothing, all shall go' (line 4). The testimony of the rocks, the fossils found in 'scarpèd cliff and quarried stone' (line 2), suggests whole species have disappeared. And the spirit, says Nature, 'does but mean the breath' (line 7); there is nothing but material existence. This horrific female Nature appears in conflict with a God whom man trusted to be loving. Man kept faith that 'God was love indeed / And love Creation's final law' (lines 13–14) even though Nature, 'red in tooth and claw' (line 15) appeared to show such faith likely to be no more than a delusive dream. Law, with all its implications of order and control, is opposed by claw, the bestial world that creates chaos. Is man, then, the speaker asks in a question which extends from stanza two to six, no more than physical matter, matter that will end up 'blown about the desert dust, / Or seal'd within the iron hills?' (lines 19–20). If this is the case, then the primeval world of the dinosaurs would seem less monstrous than man, since they at least acted in accordance with natural law, and man's life would be equally futile and frail. The only hope of any answer lies 'behind the veil' (line 28). Possibly more will be revealed after death (see Themes).

BY NIGHT WE LINGER'D ON THE LAWN (XCV)

The desire expressed in XCIII, that Hallam should 'Descend, and touch, and enter', is finally answered in this central section. The poem opens at night, with the family group gathered on the lawn.

> Some of the most striking moments in this sequence of poems come when there is some kind of undermining of boundaries – between the living and the dead, the natural and the supernatural – and this is one of the most famous of these moments. How does the opening description of the landscape prepare us for the central moment when the 'living soul was flash'd on mine' (line 36)? It is night, and so dark, but the sky is nevertheless tinged with a silvery haze of light; candles are burning, moths flicker and the white cattle glimmer. Dark is continually punctuated by light. Furthermore, there are the trees which offer an embrace and 'Laid their dark arms about the field' (line 16). The family withdraw, leaving the poet alone reading Hallam's letters once more. Tennyson's use of **paradox** here helps undermine the boundaries between the literal and the figurative as he refers to 'silent-speaking words' (lines 26–7) and 'love's dumb cry'. Consequently, when Hallam's silent words touch him from the past and, at this moment, in a trance-like state, he experiences a union, it is unclear whether the 'touch' is literal or figurative. The 'dead man' becomes 'The living soul'. Throughout the poem, the speaker's main desire has

been for renewed contact with Hallam, and this vision becomes a crucial turning point of the poem in that it provides the speaker with evidence for believing this will be possible. It suggests there is indeed life after death, that humans are more than the petty 'flies of latter spring' (L, line 10). The language of this important passage shows an emphasis on physical touch, sensation. The speaker's soul is wound up in and fused with Hallam's soul, and he hears the music of eternity. It seems as though the whole of existence is included within his experience; boundaries between spirit and matter, life and death, dissolve. Coherence, at this moment, is threatened, and we struggle to understand the meaning of 'The steps of Time – the shocks of Chance – / The blows of Death' (lines 42–3). The trance-like state ends, and the speaker is 'stricken thro' with doubt', aware of the difficulty of explaining his experience in conventional terms, in 'matter-moulded forms of speech' (line 46). His awareness of the ordinary world around him returns, and there is a movement into the new day as the dusk, also described as 'doubtful' (line 49), reveals the landscape which is then described again. Doubts, however, seem assuaged; there is a significant change in the world around him. There is now a breeze which has been 'suck'd from out the distant gloom' (line 53), a breeze that animates the whole world, brings life to all, and the section ends with the exultant announcement from the wind of the dawn of 'boundless day'. Tennyson frequently shows the work of mourning in terms of a movement from darkness into light, and it is therefore significant that this central poem begins with the word 'night' and ends with the word 'day'. And 'day' itself is shown in a new way. Compare the section VII, and its final movement into the 'blank day', with the ending of this poem, and its movement into 'boundless day'. There is a clear indication of progression in the speaker's ability to cope with his grief now that he has been given some proof of life after death (see Themes).

MAUD. A MONODRAMA (1855)

An unnamed speaker tells of his love for Maud and the feud between their families. After he kills Maud's brother in a duel, he flees to France, is confined to a madhouse, and upon being released, determines to join the army in the Crimean War

Part I begins with the speaker raging against the corruption of his age. His father had committed suicide after being financially ruined in a speculation which brought immense wealth to a neighbouring family, the family of Maud. His mother subsequently declined and died. The speaker tells of the beauty of Maud, to whom he was betrothed as a child. Maud returns to the Hall, and he attempts to remain indifferent to her, cynically rejecting the icy perfection of her beauty and remaining suspicious of her smiles. Their romance nevertheless blossoms, but Maud's brother, nicknamed the 'Sultan', disapproves; he wishes her to marry a young lord and is scornfully contemptuous of the speaker. During the brother's absence, Maud and the speaker spend a blissful day together. The brother returns and holds a grand political dinner. The first part of the poem concludes with the speaker waiting for Maud to come to him, after the dancing ends, in the garden at dawn. In Part II we are told that Maud had been followed to the garden by her brother and the young lord; there was a quarrel and the brother struck the speaker. He was seized with the impulse to avenge his father and they fought a duel. Maud's brother was killed and the speaker fled to the French coast. The great emotional strain makes him fix his gaze upon a small sea shell he finds on the shore, a shell that, although frail, has withstood the force of the seas. He is haunted by a wraith-like figure of Maud and eventually learns that she has died of grief; he has a complete mental collapse. The famous mad scene in Part II.v is set in a French asylum where he has been confined; the speaker believes he is dead and buried in a shallow grave; he hears his heart beat as the hoofs of horses overhead, and, thinking he may be only half-dead, pleads to be given peace and buried deeper. In Part III the speaker claims to have regained his sanity. A vision of Maud has appeared to him, telling him to join the army in the Crimean war, and he declares 'It is better to fight for the good than to rail at the ill' (Part III, line 57).

Finally he can be one with his kind; the country can be saved by being united in a common cause. The following commentary will first offer a brief guide to some of the most important formal and thematic issues in the poem as a whole and then provide more detailed analysis of selected sections (see also Extended Commentaries, Text 3).

Maud has been called a psychic monodrama in which, as Tennyson himself said, 'different phases of passion in one person take the place of different characters' (Memoir, 1. p. 396). These different phases of passion – tenderness and ferocity, gaiety and gloom, resentment, suspicion, and exultation – are suggested by a wide variety of verse forms and metres. There is a combination of the dramatic and the lyric, and they are put into a sequence which establishes a narrative. Even within one particular section the tone can shift abruptly. Many critics suggest there is a correspondence between form and content in this poem. The long lines of the opening section, punctuated by numerous questions and exclamations, might be said to be highly appropriate to the ranting of the speaker, for example. Others believe that there is often a striking disjunction between form and content, between how the speaker feels and how he expresses his feelings. One example which might be mentioned in support of this would be the lyric 'Strange that I felt so gay' (Part I.xx). Here the speaker is talking of the unwanted attentions forced upon Maud, but the lyric itself is light and jaunty, with its **feminine rhymes** (so gay / to-day; name him / blame him). As you read through the sections, determine the degree to which you think the striking formal variations echo or conflict with the unstable fluctuations of the speaker's mind.

It is the speaker's mind that is of central interest in this poem. Although the title might suggest Maud is the main subject, we in fact learn very little about her; she never speaks for herself and what we ultimately are presented with are the speaker's constructions of Maud. In many ways she is little more than a series of projections of his own consciousness. Initially, the speaker is unsure of her, finding her a puzzle, something 'faultily faultless' and 'splendidly null' (Part I, line 82). She is a perhaps a cheat, a coquette who will deceive him, a 'Cleopatra-like' seductress (Part I, line 216).

Once they declare their love she is sweet, 'tender and true' (Part I, line 768), a child, a blushing maiden, a bride, a woman who is, as the speaker possessively insists, 'Mine, mine by a right, from birth till death. / Mine, mine' (Part I, lines 725–6). Associated with both lily and rose, she eventually takes on two main positions: she is alternately the ideal woman or 'angel in the house' and the warrior woman, the patriot, inspiring the speaker to war with her 'martial song like a trumpet call', and 'Singing of Death, and of Honour that cannot die'(Part I, line 177). Significantly, the name Maud itself means war or battle.

War is another key issue in the poem, and *Maud* deals with various kinds of 'war'. Nature itself the speaker sees as a battlefield, a violently ruthless world at 'one with rapine', and 'The Mayfly is torn by the swallow, the sparrow spear'd by the shrike, / And the whole little wood where I sit is a world of plunder and prey' (Part I, lines 123–5). There is also, as the speaker defines it in the opening section, the **metaphorical** civil war in which the nation finds itself: this is a world driven by self-interest in which the main activities are 'cheat and be cheated' (Part I, line 32). Then there is the literal war in the Crimea which forms the focus of the conclusion (see Historical & Literary Background). Some critics read the poem as supporting the belief that the Crimean War was exactly what England needed: a means of overcoming social problems at home through providing England with a mission, uniting the nation through a worthy cause. Other critics emphasise that the apparent support for war is voiced by the speaker, not Tennyson himself. For the speaker, war is one way of redefining himself as a man, of reclaiming the identity which he has been denied by having his inheritance, his name taken from him (it is surely significant that the speaker is never named and indeed calls himself nameless). 'And ah for a man to arise in me, / That the man I am may cease to be! (Part I, lines 396–7) he declares. Can you identify the competing definitions of 'manhood' in this poem? In order to redeem himself as a man in one sense he must restrain his feminising emotions, and exercise self-mastery. He must control his rage and his hatred, his obsessions and his hysteria, and he must act in a strong and rational manner. At first he determines simply to 'bury myself in myself' (Part I, line 76), to desensitise himself by ignoring the world, but once his interest is aroused by Maud, his passion for her becomes another way through which he can redeem himself as man. When this fails, the final option is through war.

Tennyson rejected the idea that he was in any way a champion of war, and insisted that the poem was a **dramatic monologue** and the sentiments placed in the mouth of a madman. Significantly, the poem was originally called 'Maud or the Madness'. The madness of the speaker can be said to represent the greater malaise of the nation, the madness of the age. Although some critics read Parts II and III as recording the speaker's mental collapse and subsequent recovery, others debate the stage at which he can be defined as mad, and question whether he does in fact recover. There are, then, at least three different ways of reading the conclusion to *Maud*. In one reading, the speaker recovers from his madness and is finally able to enter a world where, although marked by violence and greed, there are also signs of a nobler spirit which seeks to resolve injustice; this reading would suggest an approval of war, a belief in the British mission in the Crimea, and possibly also a belief that English society could benefit from being united in a common cause. Another reading would suggest that the speaker's decision to go to war is an indication of continuing madness, and that perhaps he has been mad from the start. Certainly, the speaker always fears he may have inherited his father's tendencies, and his opening rant does not suggest a stable mind. Furthermore, if part of this nation's malaise or madness is the drive to war, then the speaker's decision to align himself with the cause is an indication of his own continuing madness. In this reading, Tennyson could be seen as criticising the war. Finally, the ending could be interpreted as the speaker, although not now mad in the conventional sense, deciding to harden himself into a new kind of insensibility by accepting the ideology of his world. In this case, Tennyson would be criticising not only the war, but the whole ideology which made that war possible.

I HATE THE DREADFUL HOLLOW BEHIND THE LITTLE WOOD (PART I.I.)

This opening section offers a combination of social commentary, natural description, and self-analysis. The poem begins with an explosive expression of emotion. The speaker tells of the suicide of his father and expresses his horror of the 'dreadful hollow' (line 1). As the harsh and dissonant language suggests, his mind, as a result of this childhood experience, has become obsessed with death and violence. From the start the speaker projects all his own obsessions upon things or people external to him. Recalling his father's death, the speaker searches for meaning, and it is the old man, who benefited from the father's downfall and who is now lord of the hall, whom he believes is to blame. The father's death and the family's resulting loss of economic and social position leaves the old man 'gorged' but the speaker 'flaccid and drain'd' (line 20). The language here suggests his resulting impotence, the loss of his identity as a 'man', and the desire to redeem himself as a man will become a driving concern. Moving to a wider assessment of the situation, he sees the condition of the nation as resembling civil war: all are motivated by self-interest. Twice he asks 'Is it peace or war?' with reference to the condition of the nation and the inequalities that exist; the blame for this condition he places on the 'ledger' (line 35), on the desire for profit. The speaker concludes it would be better by far to have a real war waged against a common enemy.

What effect is created by the extremely long lines of this opening section and by the repeated use of questions and exclamations? Does the speaker appear excited, angry? He checks himself as he realises he is 'raging alone as my father raged in his mood' (line 53) but, formally, the language continues to express rage: exclamations, questions, emphasis, and melodramatic descriptions of the 'horror of shatter'd limbs' (line 56) continue. Fearing he too may go mad and kill himself, he determines again not to brood on the past, and considers leaving 'the place and the pit and the fear' (line 64). But there are workmen at the hall, and Maud will be returning with her family. Momentarily, the form of the poem in stanza xviii becomes calmer, more harmonious, with the **anaphoric** use of the name 'Maud' and smooth, flowing lines, with alternate lines echoing the same balanced grammatical construction. But this does not last, and we are immediately returned to the fears and the questioning and a sense of fragmentation in the short jolting phrases: 'What is she now? My dreams are bad. She may bring me a curse' (line 73). This section ends with the speaker's declaration 'I will bury myself in myself, and the Devil may pipe to his own' (line 76). In a sense, he is deciding to reproduce his father's actions, to leave the world behind, to achieve some state of insensibility. This desire to 'bury' the self reappears frequently throughout the poem and will become horrifically fulfilled later in the asylum, by the experience of believing himself buried when he is still only half-dead. (For a detailed reading of the first five stanzas of this section see Extended Commentaries, Text 3.)

Echo in classical myth, Echo was a nymph in love with Narcissus; her love unreturned, she pined away until only her voice was left

Cain the son of Adam and Eve, Cain killed his brother Abel (Genesis 4:5)

Mammonite Mammon refers to the gods of this world, specifically riches; the Victorian thinker Carlyle identified Mammon as the god of industrial capitalism

Timour also known as Tamberlane, a Tartan conqueror (1336–1405) credited with numerous atrocities

three-decker a warship with three gun decks

COME INTO THE GARDEN, MAUD (PART I.XXII.)

In this last section of Part I, which will be followed by the duel and the separation of the lovers, the narrator expresses his joy as he waits for Maud in her garden. He hears the music from the ballroom within, and longs for Maud to leave the dancing and join him.

Do you hear the echo of a once popular dance in the rising rhythms of the lines here? Rather appropriately considering the context, the lines echo the rhythms of a polka. The critics have had quite conflicting responses to this section, some finding it an expression of a disordered mind and some even find it quite laughable; the majority, however, consider it to be an intense and magical expression of love. This section is full of sensuous and unusual images and sensations, full of, colour and light and movement. How do you respond to the **metaphor** which describes night as a 'black bat' (line 851)? Is this an appropriate and forceful image or do you think it is an indication of the still strange state of the speaker's mind? Spices and perfumes waft on the air, and the sun is beginning to rise; the world is transformed and animated by the speaker's desire and his anticipation. Even death, which has previously absorbed him, is transformed into something else, robbed of its negative connotations. Drawing upon the association of dying with sexual climax, Tennyson's speaker describes the planet of love, Venus, the morning star, starting to faint in the light 'On a bed of daffodil sky', to 'faint in the light of the sun she loves, / To faint in his light, and to die' (lines 859–61).

The music from the ballroom is no longer heard, and silence falls. At this point, the speaker turns to speak to the flowers. Tennyson is drawing upon the conventions of Persian love poetry. How do you respond to the speaker's insistent '"But mine, but mine", so I sware to the rose, / "For ever and ever, mine"' (lines 880–1)? There seems to be something rather dangerous in this aggressive insistence on possession. It may even echo the demands of the self-interested, profit-driven society that the speaker scorns. But in other ways this seems to be a world quite separate, a new Eden. The word 'blood', like death itself, has been tamed, robbed of its negative connotations, and becomes indicative purely of passion: 'And the soul of the rose went into my blood' (line 882). Red, in its associations with roses, similarly now seems to have little to do with death, and also becomes suggestive of sexual passion. If the dominant imagery here draws upon flowers, in particular the rose and the lily, **symbolic** of passion and purity, then Maud herself, 'Queen lily and rose in one' (line 905), combines the two.

On one level, this section, particularly stanza x, does perhaps seem to invite the **parodic** treatment it was given by Lewis Carroll in *Alice Through the Looking Glass*: 'She's coming!' cried the Larkspur. 'I hear her footstep, thump, thump, thump …'. On the other hand, the lines beautifully capture the speaker's growing excitement and anticipation and lead skilfully on to the surprising change in a resounding final stanza. One critic has suggested that the last four stanzas of this section are almost delirious, and in the final stanza the speaker is quite off balance. However, this climactic expression of the speaker's passion for Maud is surely nevertheless intensely moving and thrilling, a moment of complete rapture before the collapse of all hope in Part II. The speaker's desire is so intense that he imagines that even after death his passion will persist, his body will respond to her presence.

What happens in this last stanza (xi) and why does it seem so different from the previous stanzas in this section? While in the magical world just created, the speaker seems to have rejected any negative suggestions of blood or death, the language of passion and desire is frequently fused with the language of violence and aggression in this poem, and now there is a return to such a fusion. As the speaker imagines his dust beating, and trembling under her feet, and blossoming in 'purple and red' (line 923), flowers mix with blood, desire with death. Much of this section, with its polka rhythms and its flowery language suggestive of the Victorian parlour, comes close to a rather cloying sentimentality. But the language changes notably at the end and cloying sentiment is replaced by something forceful, passionate, violent:

My heart would hear her and beat
  Were it earth in an earthy bed;
My dust would hear her and beat,
  Had I lain for a century dead,
Would start and tremble under her feet,
  And blossom in purple and red. (lines 918–923)

Why is there such a startling change? In 'Nation, Class, and Gender: Tennyson's *Maud* and War' (in Rebecca Stott, ed. *Tennyson*, Longman, 1996), Joseph Bristow has shown that, with *Maud*, we are in a world with many conflicting constructions of the masculine and feminine and here, in this love song, there are two ideologies working on the hero, and on his representation of Maud (see Themes). She is, on the one hand, the Angel in the House, the sweet passive woman. But this is also a poem about war, and Maud is associated also with martial songs and with nationalism. Similarly, the speaker is both the sentimental lover and the militant soldier. So, in the first part of this section, we have the flowery language of love appropriate to the former, and in the final stanza we have the beat of the drum, violence, passion and death, the soul blossoming in 'purple and red'.

Do you think that this image of being 'earth in an earthy bed' (line 919) echoes and anticipates any other moments in the poem. There is, for example, the speaker's initial decision to 'bury myself in myself' in the opening section, and the later horrific delusion in the asylum (Part II.v), the belief that he has been buried alive. In order to get the full sense of the frenzy of sexual passion that is conveyed by this section of the poem, you may find it useful to compare it with another beautiful love lyric 'I have led her home, my love, my only friend' (Part I.xviii). This variation on an **epithalamion**, with many echoes of the Song of Songs, is full of the calm and peace of contentment; a comparison of the language of these two poems will reveal much about how these contrasting effects are achieved.

DEAD, LONG DEAD (PART II.V.)

This section of the poem is set in the madhouse, and the speaker is under the delusion that he is dead and buried. The language here echoes the language in the final stanza of 'Come into the garden, Maud' (Part I.xxii) as the speaker imagines 'my heart is a handful of dust, / And the wheels go over my head, / And my bones are shaken with pain' (lines 241–3). He believes he has been buried, and hears the beating of his own heart as the traffic above the grave. Repetition emphasises the idea of pounding horse hooves, and the endless feet, 'Driving, hurrying, marrying, burying' (line 250). While he had once equated death with peace, he now believes there is 'no peace in the grave' (line 254). This madhouse seems like a microcosm of the outer world. The other inhabitants of the asylum, whom he sees as other dead men who are chattering and wandering to and fro, are similarly obsessed with one particular proposition and act as though they were corrupt lords, politicians, or doctors in the 'normal' world. Everything is emptied of its meaning for him, the world itself, in which 'churches have kill'd their Christ' (line 267) and statesmen betray their party's secrets to the press, has gone mad.

Additionally, everything that he once believed in is shown to be a lie. He recalls the scene of 'Come into the garden, Maud' (Part I.xxii), and there is a terrifying change in the implications of what he once saw and transformed into something magical. The moment, he now sees, was productive of nothing, 'It is only flowers, they had no fruits' (line 315). Indeed, though once stripped of their negative connotations, he now fears the red roses were 'not roses, but blood' (line 316). Maud, who has never anyway been for us anything more than a construction of the speaker, is the one thing notably 'silent' (line 306) in this world of noise; he imagines her as a ghost standing at his head, she is one who 'never speaks her mind' and is 'Not beautiful now, not even kind' (lines 304–5).

What is most significant here is that the speaker seems to have lost the power to shape and transform his world; instead it seems to control him. This might suggest that nothing retains meaning; language has lost significance; it is 'chatter' (line 257) and 'blabbing' (line 274); there is 'Nothing but idiot gabble!' (line 279). And yet perhaps it is that he knows too much now, here where 'Everything came to be known' (line 289); he has become too aware of the corruption of the world and it is this corruption which is the 'idiot gabble'. If this is the case, then he longs to be protected from this knowledge; he wants to be buried so deep he will no longer be aware of it: 'somebody, surely, some kind heart will come / To bury me, bury me / Deeper, ever so little deeper' (lines 341–3).

Herbert Tucker believes that the answer to this prayer comes in Part III, in what he calls 'the hero's defection into lobotomized jingoism' (*Tennyson and the Doom of Romanticism*, Harvard University Press, 1988, p. 429). Only by accepting an immersion in his culture, and his culture's ideals, can the speaker can end his unbearable awareness: 'I have felt with my native land, I am one with my kind' he concludes; 'I embrace the purpose of God, and the doom assigned' (Part III, lines 58–9). As Tucker observes, 'the merciful ground of culture has opened to swallow the hero up, and he has fallen into the bliss of the state' (p. 428).

TITHONUS (1860)

Tithonus, gifted with immortality but not perpetual youth, longs to be released from the burden of life

This poem is based on the myth of Tithonus, a mortal loved by the goddess of the dawn, Aurora or Eos; she gave him eternal life but forgot to give him eternal youth. In the myth, the gods eventually take pity upon him and turn him into a grasshopper, but there is no hint of this solution in Tennyson's poem. Spoken by Tithonus himself, this **dramatic monologue** alternates between expressions of present despair and memories of past happiness. He begins by describing the cycles of life and death that he sees all around him; he only is excluded from this natural process. He has withered away to become no more than a white-haired shadow. He then recalls the time when he was young and beloved of Eos; he asked for immortality, and she granted his request. The 'strong Hours' (line 18) then wasted him; though they could not kill him, they left him 'maim'd' (line 20). 'Let me go,' he asks, 'take back thy gift' (line 27). Tithonus describes the dawn rising. Aurora remains silent and her tears frighten him as they suggest she has no power to rescind her gift. He recalls how differently he felt about her presence before when she bathed him in the warmth of her love. Now he begs to be released from this love: 'How can my nature longer mix with thine?' (line 65) he asks, and hopefully anticipates the moment when he will be returned to the earth and forget the courts of dawn and Eos herself.

Tennyson saw 'Tithonus' as a pendant to 'Ulysses'. While the latter expresses the ever unsatisfied yearning for more, the former expresses a desire for oblivion, suggesting that sometimes mundane life is preferable. We are immediately alerted to the dominant mood of this poem by the opening lines:

The woods decay, the woods decay and fall,
The vapours weep their burthen to the ground,
Man comes and tills the field and lies beneath,
And after many a summer dies the swan.
Me only cruel immortality
Consumes: (lines 1–6)

The repetition in the first line, along with the emphatic **caesura**, immediately suggest weariness. There are no variations in the **iambic pentameters** of the first four lines: the pace is regular and almost plodding. The **end-stopped** lines emphasise the need to pause. We could say that all these points function to create the appropriate voice for this weary and withered man. On the other hand, we could also say that the regularity creates a sense of quiet harmony and balance that reflects the harmony Tithonus sees within the natural cycle of life from which he is excluded. In that case, the sudden wrenching awkwardness in 'Me only cruel immortality / Consumes' (lines 5–6) could convey how Tithonus feels himself at odds with this harmony. Why do you think there is such a disturbing inversion of syntax in these lines? It is probably important that the inversion leads to a stress on 'Me', as Tithonus is – naturally – quite self-pitying, absorbed by his predicament. The **enjambment** is similarly disturbing, after the four previous lines, self-contained, end-stopped units. To see just how skilfully Tennyson achieves his effects, it is worth while comparing these lines with the opening lines of 'Tithon', an earlier and shorter version of this poem:

Ay me! ay me! the woods decay and fall,
The vapours weep their substance to the ground,
Man comes and tills the earth and lies beneath,
And after many summers dies the rose.
Me only fatal immortality
Consumes.

The opening words here doubly stress the emphasis on the self (I/me, I/me), but the use of repetition in our later version is much more effective in conveying weariness. Purely from the perspective of sound, why do you think Tennyson eventually preferred 'burthen' to 'substance' and 'swan' to 'rose'? The use of swan adds **alliterative** effect to the line, while the use of 'burthen' is far more effective in suggesting heaviness, weight, than 'substance'. Overall, there is little formal variation in this poem. At one point, however, as Tithonus recalls the passionate relationship he had with Eos, the metre does become more vigorous; between lines 50 and 63, **trochees** and **spondees** sometimes substitute for **iambs**; now there are few end-stopped lines; past vitality is echoed and reproduced in the lines, suggesting that Tithonus is agitated by these memories.

The words 'Ay me! ay me!' which Tennyson eliminates as the opening in the final version are transferred to the moment when Tithonus recalls the past: 'Ay me! ay me! with what another heart / In days far-off, and with what other eyes / I used to watch – if I be he that watch'd –' (lines 50–2). The ay/me suggests a split in Tithonus; the man he is now is quite distinct from the man he was. This split within him is also suggested when he describes himself as 'this gray shadow, once a man – / So glorious in his beauty and thy choice, / Who madest him thy chosen, that he seem'd / To his great heart none other than a God!' (lines 11–14). The choice of the pronoun here is telling, as 'I' becomes 'he'. The man who now withers away seems to have little connection with this glorious being. And yet Tithonus has clearly not fully accepted the eternal nature of his present condition: 'Why wilt thou ever scare me with thy tears' (line 46) he asks Eos, implying he still believes she might be able to give him release, to restore him to mortality.

How does Tennyson draw upon colour to suggest both the contrast between past and present and the conflict between the world of Eos in which Tithonus is confined and the world of men to which he longs to return? The golds and silvers of the dawn are offset by the browns and greens of the earth. The glowing crimson of passion in the past is similarly offset by the white and grey shadow that Tithonus has become. Decay is the focus of both the beginning and the ending of the poem, decay associated with the world of mortality. In between, there is the shining immortal world of the goddess. It would be too simple to suggest Tithonus is concerned now only with the first, and so it is questionable whether the poem is, as some critics suggest, simply an exploration of the impulse to suicide. Tithonus may be partly consumed by a desire for death, but he continues to remember and yearn also for the lost passionate days he knew with Eos. He has lost both, and longs for both. You should be able to find numerous other contrasting words and images that convey the distinctions between the two worlds, the world of mortals and mortality, and the world of the goddess and immortality, that suggest a tension between Tithonus's desire for death and his desire for the goddess.

Ilion Troy; according to Greek myth, Troy was a city built to the music of the god Apollo

PART THREE

CRITICAL APPROACHES

THEMES

ISOLATION & SOCIAL ENGAGEMENT

Much of Tennyson's poetry expresses the tension between the impulse to withdraw and the opposing recognition of the need for social engagement. It is sometimes suggested that the primarily lyric poetry of the early work, *Poems, Chiefly Lyrical* of 1830, focuses more upon the attraction of withdrawal and isolation and that Tennyson then abandons this self-indulgent **Romanticism** after being encouraged by the critics to deal with relevant contemporary issues. He turns away from lyric to produce the first of his **dramatic monologues**, and simultaneously turns to a more socially engaged poetry, marked by a new moral sensibility. Throughout his poetic career, however, Tennyson's poetry concerns the tension between the desire to withdraw from and engage with the world; this can be seen in such poems as 'The Lady of Shalott', 'Ulysses' and *Maud* (see Commentaries). Tennyson's awareness of the necessity of reconciling the needs of the self with the needs of society can be seen in the way his poetry gradually moves to use the personal and subjective to consider issues of wider relevance; this is done most notably in *In Memoriam* where his grief at the death of his friend leads to an interest in contemporary science and to explorations of religious faith and doubt.

SCIENCE & RELIGION

Tennyson's most important engagement with contemporary science occurs in *In Memoriam*, an elegy on the death of his friend Arthur Hallam, and written between 1833 and 1850. Drawing partly upon the theories of Charles Lyell in his *The Principles of Geology* (1833), Tennyson here anticipates Darwin's theory of evolution as outlined in *On the Origin of Species* (1859). Scientific theories of the time undermined conventional religious beliefs in two main ways. First, they showed that the earth had been created long before the time suggested by biblical accounts of creation. Second, they suggested that the human race, far from being the perfected and complete creation of a kindly God who made the world for their benefit alone, was just one more element in a world of total flux and was caught up, like all beings, in the processes of evolution. The hope, as expressed in *In Memoriam*, is that humanity might 'Move upward, working out the beast / And let the ape and tiger die' (CXVIII, lines 27–8). But evolution did not necessarily mean progress; it could mean simply a struggle leading to extinction or, even worse, there was always the possibility that mankind would devolve instead: at the end of the *Idylls of the King*, for example, Arthur laments his realm as it 'Reels back into the beast' ('The Passing of Arthur', line 26). More generally, Tennyson did seem to adopt a type of evolutionary view. He recognised change as inevitable and stagnation to be 'more dangerous than Revolution' (*Memoir*, ii. p. 339). And so in the 'Morte d'Arthur', Arthur tells Bedivere: 'The old order changeth, yielding place to new, / And God fulfils himself in many ways, / Lest one good custom should corrupt the world' (lines 240–2).

Nevertheless, for Tennyson, as for many Victorians, the scientific discoveries of the time provoked a crisis of religious faith. He stresses mankind's continuing need to believe, but also those issues which make it difficult to do so. Tennyson has lost any firm ground for belief in his God, and ultimately has to base his faith not on external evidence but on inner experience. In section CXXIV of *In Memoriam* he writes 'I found Him not in world or sun, / Or eagle's wing, or insect's eye' (lines 5–6), but when his faith falters and a rational voice appears to cry 'believe no more' (line 10), then feeling overrides the 'freezing reason's colder part' (line 14), and 'like a man in wrath the heart / Stood up and answered "I have felt"' (lines 15–16). Tennyson can ultimately accept the idea of evolution, and the implication that mankind may become extinct, because he believes that God will replace the species with another, with a higher, and more spiritual type of mankind which he sees as being foreshadowed by Hallam: The 'herald of a higher race', a 'noble type' (Epilogue, line 138), the perfected being into which the race will evolve. *In Memoriam* consequently becomes a relatively optimistic poem. In contrast, the *Idylls of the King*, by dramatising the ultimate failure of Arthur and his knights of the Round Table, and showing the loss of the ideal when mankind fails to keep faith, appears more pessimistic. Nevertheless, some hope can be found in the figure of Bedivere, the last knight who will take the ideals into the new age (see also Historical & Literary Background).

NATURE

For the earlier **Romantic** poets, nature was both a source of imaginative inspiration and a moral guide. Scientific discoveries in the Victorian age not only led to a crisis of faith, they also made it difficult to maintain the Romantic valorisation of nature. In section LVI of *In Memoriam*, Tennyson replaces the Romantic view of nature as benevolent nurse and guide with a ferocious nature 'red in tooth and claw' (line 15). The testimony of geological discoveries, the fossils found in 'scarpèd cliff and quarried stone' (line 2), suggests whole species have disappeared, and that nature, who shrieks 'I care for nothing, all shall go' (line 4) has no love for mankind, no kindly maternal feelings at all. In other works, Tennyson tends to use nature, and exterior landscapes generally, to suggest more about the state of the observer than the state of what is observed (see Language & Style).

THE PAST

Tennyson was, throughout his life, haunted by what he called 'the passion of the past' ('The Ancient Sage', line 220). Initially, critics tended to interpret this as nostalgia, as a passion for what is lost and gone. The theme of loss, these critics suggest, is Tennyson's major source of imaginative energy: he is primarily an elegiac poet, exploring above all 'the days that are no more'. This does not mean, however, that Tennyson is necessarily a nostalgic poet, and many critics would now argue that he is more interested in the *consequences* of loss than he is in the past itself. He explores, for example, the ways in which we may respond to loss, as in 'Mariana', the actual process of remembering, as in 'Break, break, break', and the **paradoxical** presence of what is absent within the act of recollection, as in 'Tears, Idle Tears' (see Commentaries). The past is also important for Tennyson to the extent that the events of the past continue to have significance for the present; this can be particularly seen through his participation in the nineteenth-century medieval revival.

This revival was not a nostalgic attempt to escape the industrialised world by idealising the past, but an attempt to reform the industrial world. All the Victorian writers who reconstruct the medieval past in their writings, including Thomas Carlyle in *Past and Present* (1843) and John Ruskin in 'Nature of Gothic' (1853), are concerned with reform. Tennyson's medieval poems also use the past to engage with contemporary issues. The *Idylls of the King*, for example, deals with the need to keep faith in one's ideals, a significant issue in an age riven by religious doubt, and it contains a relevant message and warning for the Victorian world in its tracing of the decline of a community, in its presentation of a once healthy social order gradually diseased by corruption and lack of faith.

POLITICS

Is Tennyson, as some critics believe, the imperialist poet whose pen was used to further the cause of the British Empire? The epilogue to *Idylls of the King* celebrates 'Our ocean-empire with her boundless homes / For ever-broadening England' ('To the Queen', lines 29–30), while 'The Defence of Lucknow' celebrates the 'English in heart and in limb, / Strong with the strength of the race to command, to obey, to endure' (lines 46–47). Many of Tennyson's contemporaries reacted with horror to what they saw as Tennyson's glorification of war in *Maud*, but it must be remembered that these ideas are expressed by a dramatised speaker, not Tennyson, and this speaker's belief that war might solve the problems of the country could be just one more sign of his madness. Tennyson undeniably felt admiration for those who went to war in defence of Britain, but it was more the heroism of the soldier rather than any false ideals about war which seems to have impressed him. In 'The Charge of the Light Brigade', the praise of those 'Noble six hundred' (line 55) and the question 'When can their glory fade?' (line 50) must be set against the criticism implicit in that short but telling phrase, 'someone had blundered' (line 12). The dignity of the soldiers is maintained at the same time as the tactical stupidity of the suicidal action is recognised. Tennyson, overall, has a more uneasy relationship with his age than has often been admitted; he is no mouthpiece for Victorian ideology. This can also be seen in the way he reacted in such poems as *Maud* against the materialism of the society in which he lived and the appalling social and

POLITICS continued

economic conditions created by a class-conscious, money-conscious England. It can also be seen in his engagement with gender politics of the time (see Men & Women).

LOVE & MARRIAGE

As Marion Shaw has observed, Tennyson seems most 'Tennysonian' when he is writing about romantic love, about love which is obsessive, idealistic and erotic. But the presence of this kind of desire in his poetry is matched by a desire for stability and domestic happiness. Marriage is presented as an ideal, the potential source of all happiness on an individual level and stability on a social level. Marriage offers a means of overcoming the isolation of the individual. And it is a new kind of marriage that Tennyson envisions as the ideal; in *The Princess* this ideal is summarised by the Prince:

> ... in true marriage lies
> Nor equal, nor unequal: each fulfils
> Defect in each, and always thought in thought,
> Purpose in purpose, will in will, they grow,
> The single pure and perfect animal,
> The two-celled heart beating, with one full stroke,
> Life (VII. lines 284–9)

Romantic desire and the desire for domestic stability, however, seem strangely incompatible in Tennyson's poetry, and marriages repeatedly fail. Only in *The Princess* does romantic love translate successfully into marriage. Significantly, the romances of most of Tennyson's lovers have their source in an early childhood attachment. It is within the adult world that these attachments fail. During Tennyson's earlier and middle period it is usually social and economic conditions, problems within the external adult world, that account for the failure of marriage or the failure of romantic love to translate into marriage; this is the case, for example, in *Maud*. During his later period the problem is more frequently a failure within the marriage itself, a lack of love or trust, as in so many of the marriages in *Idylls of the King*.

MEN & WOMEN

In his early poems, such as 'Mariana' and 'The Lady of Shalott', Tennyson primarily appropriates the feminine in order to suggest a link between the feminine and the imagination or between the feminine and states of unconsciousness, associated with withdrawal from the world. Tennyson's interest in images of isolated and unhappy women has been frequently noted by the critics. Frustrated and trapped in some situation, they are distanced from the world of action: Mariana has one window through which she looks out on to the world, the Lady of Shalott sees through her mirror, Oenone in her valley sees through the gorges to Troy.

In his later works, Tennyson engages more with the position of women in Victorian England, and he became one of the first to explore the 'woman question' with *The Princess*, joining in the debate over the rights of women, women's education and women's roles. The position on male and female roles outlined by the prince in *The Princess* (quoted above in Love & Marriage) is quite different from that espoused by conventional gender ideology. The Prince's father is the spokesman for the more conservative position of Victorian patriarchy:

> Man for the field and woman for the hearth:
> Man for the sword and for the needle she;
> Man with the head and woman with the heart:
> Man to command and woman to obey;
> All else confusion (V, lines 437–41)

But this is not Tennyson's position. *The Princess* admittedly concludes with the traditional happy ending of a marriage, with the Prince telling Ida 'Accomplish thou my manhood and thyself; / Lay thy sweet hands in mine and trust to me' (VII, lines 344–5). Furthermore, Ida ultimately is transformed into a more submissive traditional wife, suggested by her change from the speaker to the listener, from the active to the passive, blushing, mild wife. However, the narrative overall allows the women to express fully their sense that they have been wronged and supports their claims for more equal rights. Here, as so often in his poetry, Tennyson subverts conventional gender ideology. Sexual difference may be reinstated by the frame of the poem and by the conclusion, but it is undercut by such things as the feminised cross-dressing males and the masculine Ida, and also by the lyrics (see Extended Commentaries, Text 1: 'Now sleeps the crimson petal').

By the mid nineteenth century, masculinity was a much contested term (see Historical & Literary Background). Tennyson engages with the debate in his exploration of competing definitions of masculinity in works like *Maud*, where the speaker desires to attain control over his violent (feminine) emotions, and calls for new kinds of masculinity: Tennyson's men tend not to be particularly 'manly' in the traditional sense. Those male figures who do display the more traditional heroic qualities of manliness are usually older men, like Ulysses, and nearing death. On the whole, Tennyson's men tend more to be uncertain, weak, passive and emotionally vulnerable. They are often moving towards the attainment of manliness, as in the case of the speaker of *Maud*, but the interest tends to lie in their present effeminate state. This is partly necessary because of Tennyson's concern with the exploration of emotional states; the self-control and restraint associated with manliness are not conducive to such explorations. There is also the fact that, particularly in Tennyson's later works, there is an insistence that men should assume more of the feminine. Alan Sinfield has suggested this is part of his attempt to offer an alternative to his own ruthlessly materialistic society. Too much of the feminine, however, must be avoided. This would seem to be the case with Tennyson's feminised King Arthur in the *Idylls*; Elliot L. Gilbert suggests that poem examines 'the advantages and dangers of sexual role reversal, with King Arthur himself playing, in a number of significant ways, the part usually assigned by culture to the woman' ('The Female King: Tennyson's Arthurian Apocalypse', *PMLA* 98.5, 1983, p. 865). Many of Tennyson's feminised males are eventually remasculinised, but the degree to which this is seen as positive is debatable and dependent upon which of the many competing versions of masculinity is attained. To what extent do you think, for example, it is a positive movement in *Maud*? *In Memoriam* explores a variety of possible gender positions, and the relationship between the speaker and Arthur Hallam is presented throughout much of the poem in terms of a conventional heterosexual relationship. The speaker is feminised through his emotional response and his state as mourner is described in such terms as widower, wife and bride. This has led many critics to claim the presence of homoerotic desire. Ultimately, however, the speaker moves towards a more mature and socialised masculinity. The hand of Hallam, which gathers more and more erotic associations as the poem proceeds, is replaced by the hand of God; feminine desire is rejected in favour of masculine wisdom; and in the Epilogue Tennyson takes on the role of giving away the bride at the wedding of his friend. Heterosexual marriage reinstates conventional sexual roles, and yet, once again, what remains in the mind are the ways in which gender ideology is subverted rather than the ways it is resolved.

POETIC FORM

Tennyson experimented with a wide range of established poetic forms and also contributed to the development of some of the new forms that emerged in the Victorian age, most notably, the **dramatic monologue**. The dramatic monologue is the name given to a kind of poem in which a speaker, not the poet, addresses a listener, not the reader. This form was perfected by Browning and Tennyson almost simultaneously in the 1840s, and its emergence is connected to both the growing interest in psychology and the reaction against the **Romantic** emphasis on self-expression (see Historical & Literary Background). In the dramatic monologue poets are clearly distanced from their poems: there is a well defined speaker, sometimes a mythical figure, like Ulysses or Tithonus, or an invented character, like the speakers in 'Locksley Hall' or *Maud*. This speaker usually addresses an auditor: Tithonus, for example, is addressing Eos, the goddess of dawn. Today we may be so familiar with the concept of **persona** that we would be unlikely to conflate the speaker of a poem with the poet writing the poem, but it was the Victorians, and particularly Tennyson and Browning, who were first responsible for emphasising the separation between the two.

Tennyson produced what is the most important **elegy** of the nineteenth century with *In Memoriam*, and this long poem consisting of 131 lyrics, with its struggle between faith and doubt, could also be considered one of the most representative, and most experimental, of Victorian poems. Tennyson rejects the conventional narrative structure of the **pastoral elegy**, introduced by Theocritus in his *Idylls*, and followed in such later major elegies as Milton's 'Lycidas' (1638) and Shelley's *Adonais*

(1821). Rather than producing an elegy which relentlessly drives the reader on from grief to recovery, Tennyson creates a poetry of fragments, of brief lyrics which more effectively capture his transitory and contradictory emotions. Links are created primarily through recurrent images and motifs, such as the hand and the house. His series of lyrics may, like other elegies, lead the reader through the conventional process of mourning – moving from grief and despair and doubt to hope and faith and eventual recovery, but not in the conventionally linear fashion: at each stage opposing emotions emerge, doubt continually undercuts faith, and grief intrudes upon moments of optimism (see also Themes, on Science & Religion).

Tennyson also wrote much narrative verse, including the 'English Idylls' of 1842, which combine a pastoral form with a contemporary setting, and *Enoch Arden*, a form of novel in verse. More notably, *Idylls of the King* takes Arthurian **romance**, retaining the improbable and magical events, but reworks it, with the addition of more modern realistic responses. This is particularly evident in the early 'The Epic' which offers a modern realistic frame to the romance of the 'Morte d'Arthur', later incorporated into the *Idylls*. While the *Idylls* is clearly linked to **epic** as well as romance, unlike traditional epics such as the *Odyssey* or the *Aeneid*, it is not limited to the story of a single hero. The twelve parts, rather than demonstrating narrative continuity, focus on a variety of characters and are linked by the focus on these characters' responses to King Arthur and his ideals. It is this combination of the improbabilities of traditional romance with psychological realism which made this poem of particular interest to Tennyson's Victorian readers.

With *The Princess*, Tennyson experimented with poetic form to create what Elaine Jordan has called, 'a hermaphrodite among poems, a thing that doesn't easily fit into a category' (*Alfred Tennyson*, Cambridge University Press, 1988, p. 83). Tennyson subtitled it 'A Medley', and it combines narrative with some of the best lyrics he ever wrote. *Maud* is similarly experimental in form, taking the dramatic monologue and combining it with lyric, turning it into a psychic monodrama, an interior drama in which, as Tennyson said, 'different phases of passion in one person take the place of different characters'. In addition to these poetic forms, Tennyson also experimented with dialect poems, including 'Northern Farmer. Old Style' and 'Northern Farmer. New Style', with

epistolary verse such as 'To E. Fitzgerald', and **odes**, including 'Ode on the Death of the Duke of Wellington'.

LANGUAGE & STYLE

It is not surprising that Tennyson inspired so many artists to transform his verbal texts into a visual medium. Tennyson is particularly skilled at suggesting pictorial effects with his language and his work has often been described as 'painterly'. Like most Victorians, Tennyson uses nature more imagistically than the **Romantics**, to suggest more about the observer than about what is observed; in his descriptions the literal is frequently blended with the figurative. His landscapes are sharply delineated, often with an almost scientific precision, but at the same time used to evoke emotional states: the concrete becomes fused with, and gives form to, the abstract. His ability to use landscape to evoke a state of mind is strikingly evident in the early 'Mariana', which offers a detailed and almost photographically accurate description of the grange and its surroundings while nevertheless using these details to convey Mariana's own feelings; the setting becomes an emanation of her consciousness.

In *Maud*, he moves further away from scientific accuracy so that the speaker's description of the 'dreadful hollow' where his father committed suicide reveals the unbalanced state of his mind. The hollow's 'lips' or edges he sees as being 'dabbled with blood-red heath' and the 'red-ribb'd ledges drip with a silent horror of blood' (Part I, lines 2–3). The speaker's reading of the landscape suggests he has become obsessed with death and violence. Tennyson also uses **pathetic fallacy** to show how the speaker sees the natural world itself partaking of the ills of a capitalistic society; the 'wind like a broken worldling wail'd' (Part I, line 11), and, echoing the society's emphasis on profit, 'the flying gold' – that is the leaves – 'of the ruin'd woodlands drove thro' the air' (Part I, line 12) (see Extended Commentaries, Text 3 for a more detailed analysis).

Tennyson's poetry reveals a wide range of styles; there is no one style that could confidently be called 'Tennysonian'. In 'The Lotos-Eaters', slumberous and luxurious language serves to express the drugged and semiconscious condition of the Lotos-eaters:

> There is sweet music here that softer falls
> Than petals from blown roses on the grass,
> Or night-dews on still waters between walls
> Of shadowy granite, in a gleaming pass;
> Music that gentlier on the spirit lies,
> Than tir'd eyelids upon tir'd eyes; (lines 46–51)

Here the soft **sibilant** 's' sound harmoniously links the lines, while the long drawn out **assonantal** sounds of 'ee' and 'ay' suggest a drowsy, sensuous delight. At the opposite end of the spectrum are the long blustering **trochaic** lines of 'Locksley Hall' as the speaker rails against his betrayal by Amy: 'Woman is the lesser man, and all thy passions, match'd with mine, / Are as moonlight unto sunlight, and as water unto wine' (lines 151–2). And these in turn contrast with the notable restraint and simplicity of 'Break, break, break, / On thy cold gray stones, O Sea!' (lines 1–2). There is the archaic language of the 'Morte d'Arthur' which contrasts with the modern idiom of its frame in 'The Epic'. Tennyson's wide range of styles is perhaps most strikingly demonstrated by *Maud*, where different phases of passion – tenderness and ferocity, gaiety and gloom, resentment, suspicion and exultation – are effectively conveyed through the varying use of language. There is, for example, the speaker's excited and melodramatic language when he recalls the finding of his father's body in the 'ghastly pit': 'Oh father! O God! was it well? – / Mangled, and flatten'd and crush'd, and dinted into the ground' (Part I, lines 6–7). Quite different is the **tone** conveyed by the quiet and controlled language of the beautiful love song 'I have led her home, my love, my only friend' (Part I, xviii), with its repeated expression of wonder: 'There is none like her, none'. Even within one particular lyric the language and resulting tone can shift abruptly and it is necessary to be always aware of what these shifts might signify (see Commentaries).

IMAGERY

In accord with Tennyson's general tendency towards highly visual language, his imagery is most often used to present abstract ideas in highly concrete and visual forms. At times this is achieved through the use of **personification**, as so frequently in *In Memoriam*, where Time is 'a maniac scattering dust' (L, line 7), Life 'a Fury slinging flame' (L, line 8), Nature a shrieking female monster, rejecting her nurturing role (LVI), and where Tennyson asks for Sorrow to live with him as his wife (LIX) or for 'Love' to 'clasp Grief lest both be drown'd' (I). Alternately, **metaphor** often functions to link abstract with concrete, as when Tennyson asserts 'Love is and was my Lord and King' (CXXVI). This image provides a clear example of an *explicit metaphor*, with the two parts clearly distinct. The *tenor*, or subject of the metaphoric combination, is explicitly stated to be love, while the *vehicle*, or metaphoric word which carries over its meaning, is explicitly identified as 'Lord and King'. However, Tennyson more characteristically uses *implicit metaphors*, as when the speaker in *Maud* refers to Maud's 'cold and clear-cut face' (Part I, line 79), indirectly linking her to a jewel. Or he uses metaphors where the tenor and vehicle are fused. When the speaker of *In Memoriam* pleads with Hallam to 'Be near me when my light is low' (L, line 1) for example, the light may be a literal light, so that he appears like a child fearing the dark when the candle has burned down. However, it may also be a figurative light, the abstract light of his spirit. The adjective 'low' is applicable to both and the figurative and literal tend to merge. Frequently, with Tennyson's metaphorical language, the tenor is simply absent. When the speaker, mourning the absence of Hallam from the 'dark house' in *In Memoriam* describes the arrival of dawn, 'ghastly thro' the drizzling rain / On the bald street breaks the blank day' (VII, lines 11–12), there is really nothing to suggest we should link his state of mind directly with the scene, but we do, and the landscape therefore begins to assume **symbolic** qualities.

Tennyson also makes effective use of recurrent images, particularly in his longer works. The *Idylls of the King* is structured by the images of seasons. *In Memoriam* draws upon such recurrent images as the ship, the door, hand, the tree and the house to provide an essential grounding and structure to what could otherwise be an introspective and abstractly intellectual poem (see Extended Commentaries, Text 2 for an analysis of a lyric which uses both hand and house). The speaker's changing use of these images provides an indication of his changing responses to Hallam's death. *Maud*, appropriately for a poem in which the speaker is obsessed by the destructive materialism of his age, draws upon political and economic imagery. The colour red is one of many images that recur in

Maud, and variously takes on the connotations of blood and passion, depending upon the speaker's state of mind. Tennyson's recurrent images, then, tend to work through pointing out connections but at the same time differences.

SOUND PATTERNS

Tennyson has sometimes been accused of being more concerned with sound than sense, but in fact, with Tennyson, it is usually difficult to separate sound and sense in such a simple manner. Sometimes, sound patterns are used to draw the reader's attention to the connections between the words. A relatively straightforward example comes in *In Memoriam* when the speaker notes 'In words, like weeds, I'll wrap me o'er' (V, line 9), where the link between words and weeds is indicated not only by the **simile** but also by the **alliteration**. Tennyson also relies frequently upon sound patterning to suggest mood, and the sound of the words usually conveys the sense as, if not more, effectively than the actual meaning of the words. In the 'Morte d'Arthur', for example, as Bedivere carries Arthur to the lake, his efforts are skilfully suggested by the sounds of the language used to describe the landscape:

> Dry clash'd his harness in the icy caves
> And barren chasms, and all to left and right
> The bare black cliff clang'd round him, as he based
> His feet on juts of slippery crag that rang
> Sharp-smitten with the dint of armèd heels – (lines 186–90)

The sound patterns created by such alliterative groupings as clashed – chasms – cliff – clanged – crag are suggestive of harshness and the difficulties Bedivere encounters. The description is not only visual but aural: we hear the clash of the armour among the echoing cliffs and the ringing of his heels on the crags. When Bedivere finally arrives at their destination, the successful conclusion of his struggle is indicated as the scene is transformed into something beautiful and harmonious, and again this is conveyed through sound patterns, with the alliterative 'l' and the use of longer vowel sounds: 'And on a sudden, lo! the level lake, / And the long glories of the winter moon' (lines 191–2). Tennyson also makes skilful use of **onomatopoeia**, most famously in one of the songs from *The Princess*, 'Come down, O maid, from yonder mountain height'. The shepherd urges the maid to come down into the valley, where 'every sound is sweet' (line 28), and the language of the final three lines then demonstrates the point, evoking the very sounds which are being described: 'Myriads of rivulets hurrying thro' the lawn, / The moan of doves in immemorial elms, / And murmuring of innumerable bees' (lines 29–31).

Another kind of sound patterning is created through Tennyson's frequent use of the **refrain**. These refrains are always functional. In 'Mariana', for example, the use of her repeated complaint 'I am aweary, aweary, / I would that I were dead' serves to emphasise that repetition is the driving principle of Mariana's existence. Conversely, the refrain in 'The Lady of Shalott' suggests not stasis and repetition but movement and progression. The middle line of each stanza focuses upon either Camelot or Lancelot, while the last line of each stanza focuses upon Shalott and the Lady. This **paradoxically** serves not only to separate but also to link Camelot and Shalott, anticipating the moment when the lady will leave her tower of Shalott and float down to the other world of Camelot. The refrain also serves a functional purpose at the crucial point in the poem, immediately before the Lady leaves the web to look out upon Camelot. At this moment, Lancelot intrudes upon her space not only by becoming part of her world but also formally by taking over her place in the refrain, and the stanza ends not with a reference to the Lady of Shalott, but with '"Tirra lirra," by the river / Sang Sir Lancelot' (lines 107–8). The significant change in the refrain draws attention to and emphasises this moment when the two worlds begin to collide.

Other types of repetition create sound patterns with varying effects. *In Memoriam*, as Alan Sinfield has shown in his study of its language, uses a limited range of vowels and consonants in any one section, so their repetition creates patterns horizontally, within individual lines or vertically, within stanzas or whole lyrics. Furthermore, **parallelism** with respect to phrases and clauses is frequently used, as when 'Be near me when ...' is used in the first line of each stanza in Lyric L. All these devices echo one of the main concerns of the poem as a whole: the desire for connection or relatedness. Repetition can have a calm, even a mesmerising effect, as in 'The Lotos-Eaters' where 'The Lotos blooms below the barren peak: / The Lotos blows by every winding creek' (lines 145–6). Both the opening stanzas and the Choric Song of the mariners are predominantly characterised by **anaphora** and other correspondences of word and phrase, and this is particularly appropriate for men who have rejected change and action for a life of calm and stasis. Repetition can also be used to create intensity and emphasis. In 'The Lady of Shalott', when the lady leaves her loom, the use of anaphora results in a sense of building up towards an inevitable moment which intensifies the sense of crisis:

> She left the web, she left the loom,
> She made three paces thro' the room,
> She saw the water-lily bloom,
> She saw the helmet and the plume.
>   She look'd down to Camelot.
> Out flew the web and floated wide; (lines 109–14)

In these lines, a sense of growing crisis is also created by Tennyson's skilful metrical variations. In the 'The Lady of Shalott', Tennyson generally uses **trochees**, but, in the lines quoted above, he initially replaces the trochees with a regular **iambic tetrameter**. The iambic tetrameter, along with the repetition, creates a feeling of impending doom and a driving movement on to the moment of crisis when 'She look'd down to Camelot'. In this line, as the lady seals her fate, there is a significant variation with two stressed syllables (look'd down). Then, there is a striking change: the momentous effects of the lady looking are emphasised with the use of a resounding opening trochee: 'Out flew the web and floated wide'.

PART FOUR

EXTENDED COMMENTARIES

TEXT 1 'NOW SLEEPS THE CRIMSON PETAL, NOW THE WHITE' (from *THE PRINCESS*)

'Now sleeps the crimson petal, now the white;
Nor waves the cypress in the palace walk;
Nor winks the gold fin in the porphyry font:
The fire-fly wakens: waken thou with me.

Now droops the milkwhite peacock like a ghost,
And like a ghost she glimmers on to me.

Now lies the Earth all Danaë to the stars,
And all thy heart lies open unto me.

Now slides the silent meteor on, and leaves
A shining furrow, as thy thoughts in me.

Now folds the lily all her sweetness up,
And slips into the bosom of the lake:
So fold thyself, my dearest, thou, and slip
Into my bosom and be lost in me.'

The Princess is a poem concerned above all with gender conflict and sexual difference. The story concerns a prince who has been betrothed to the Princess Ida since birth. She announces she will not marry and, believing women are equal to men although treated like children, she founds a women's university with an inscription over the entrance: 'Let no man enter in on pain of death.' The Prince and two friends disguise themselves as women and gain access to the university. They are invited to join an academic expedition and eventually are revealed to be men. The women flee, and Princess Ida falls in a river only to be saved by the Prince; she is nevertheless still adamant that the men must die. The Prince's father sends an army as does the Princess's brother. There is a tournament and the Prince is injured; Ida nurses him back to health, falls in love with him, and the tale ends happily with their marriage. *The Princess* may ultimately reinstate relatively conventional ideas of true masculinity and femininity, but sexual difference is undermined throughout by such things as male crossdressing, the feminised and passive nature of the prince and female independence.

The lyric chosen for analysis here, the first of two songs Ida reads by the bed of the injured Prince after she has recognised her love for him, engages with precisely the kind of gender mixing which is found in the narrative by which it is framed. However, unlike the narrative, the lyric delights in this mixing rather than attempting to resolve it, and the focus throughout is on unity, as all oppositions, not just those of masculine and feminine, are eventually undermined, and the overall effect is of blending and enfolding of one into another. It is also a highly erotic lyric, and on the basis of your understanding of the poem you might want to consider how much validity there is in the claim of one of Tennyson's recent biographers, Robert Bernard Martin, that there is a very low level of sexual feeling both in Tennyson himself and in his work.

In form, the poem is a variation on the Persian **ghazal**; this is a short lyric which uses a single final word at regular intervals to produce a form of rhyme, focuses on amatory matters, and has a series of standard images including roses, lilies, peacocks, stars and cypresses. It also draws upon the *carpe diem* tradition, as the speaker, apparently male, is attempting to persuade a female auditor to give in to love, in much the same way as the speaker of the other lyric read by Ida, 'Come down, O maid' (see Commentaries). However, it is significant that it is read by a woman, and read in the presence of a man, if not directed specifically to him. This reinforces Tennyson's idea that men and women need to incorporate each other's positive qualities. It is also notable that Tennyson eliminates all the aggressive elements that tend to underlie the *carpe diem* poem. The speakers in such poems often attempt to persuade through threats. This is the main tactic, for example, in two famous seventeenth-century *carpe diem* poems with which you may be familiar: Robert Herrick's 'To the Virgins to Make Much of Time' and Andrew Marvell's 'To his Coy Mistress'. The speaker of the former urges

> Gather ye rosebuds while ye may,
> Old Time is still a-flying,

And this same flower that smiles today
Tomorrow will be dying.

The speaker of the latter, even more disturbingly, reminds his mistress that 'The grave's a fine and private place, / But none, I think, do there embrace.' Tennyson's lyric may be one of persuasion, and framed by imperatives – 'waken thou with me' and 'fold thyself, my dearest, thou, and slip / Into my bosom and be lost in me' – but the overall effect of the poem is extremely tender.

Formally, there is a striking sense of gentle unity about the lyric. The sense of enfolding and blending that is a thematic focus ('So fold thyself') is clearly enacted through the structural patterning, with the two four-line stanzas enfolding and framing the three couplets, and with each stanza beginning with 'Now' and ending with 'me'. Unity is also suggested through the soft but nevertheless insistent sound patterning. Herbert Tucker has shown the extent to which the lyric as a whole generates itself out of the sounds of its first verb 'sleeps'. At least one of the sounds in this word, 's' 'l' 'ee' and 'p' appears in every following verb, including waves, winks, droops, glimmers, lies, slides, leaves, until, in the final couplet, all three consonants are repeated as 'sleeps' becomes 'slips'. You should be able to find the recurrent use of these clustered consonants throughout the poem, not only in the verbs. Do you think it would be taking the analysis too far to suggest, as does Tucker, that the insistence of the patterning 'may finally evoke in the reader allied words – lips, slopes, lapse, pillows, pulse, bliss – words it never has to mention in order to enlist their suggestiveness'? (*Tennyson and the Doom of Romanticism* Harvard University Press, 1988, pp. 369–70).

The lyric is, very clearly, sexually suggestive, and yet has nothing in the least bit salacious or crude about it. Everything potentially offensive is purged and rendered harmless and the overall effect is of a gentle eroticism rather than an aggressive lewdness. This is particularly evident in the brilliant image of the third stanza 'Now lies the Earth all Danaë to the stars, / And all thy heart lies open unto me.' In classical mythology, the King of Argos was told his daughter's son would put him to death and so he resolved that she, Danaë, should never marry and locked her up in an inaccessible tower. The god Zeus, ever resourceful, metamorphosed into a shower of gold in order to gain access to Danaë and rape her. The speaker, then, is poised to enter the heart of the lady, as Zeus's golden rain entered Danaë. But do you find any indications of the lust and violence of the original story in this couplet or has Tennyson transformed the story to create something much more tenderly erotic? Christopher Ricks is particularly interesting on this couplet. He notes that to "'lie all Danaë to the stars" is to give Danaë the force of an adjective, some such epithet as "wide-open"' and the word 'open' then surfaces in the next line, in such a way, he says, that '"heart" therefore becomes – well not a euphemism, but not all that the lover yearns for. It was not Danaë's heart that was open to Jupiter. Yet to put it like this is to encourage the snigger which Tennyson totally excluded' (*Tennyson*, Macmillan, 1989, p. 193). As Ricks suggests, by turning the traditional gold shower into starlight, replacing the lecherous god with the pure stars, Tennyson creates a wonderful expression of love, rather than lust.

The idea of difference and opposition is suggested throughout the lyric, but these oppositions tend to be merged, blended, so that one becomes implicit in the other. In the opening stanza, for example, the crimson flower of passion is set against the white flower of purity. However, such an opposition is ultimately undercut by the whole thrust of the lyric, which so effectively combines what is erotic and passionate with what is chaste and pure. There is also the idea of sleeping and awakening in the first stanza, with the passive set against the active, but these two also merge. The lyric begins with 'Now sleeps', and then, in the next two lines, 'Now' is replaced by 'Nor'. Because of the exact **parallelism** of the words, we might first think this is a misprint. However, what Tennyson has skilfully managed to do with this change in construction is to incorporate the active into the passive. If he had said, for example, 'Now the cypress is still in the palace walk' or 'Now the gold fin is still in the porphyry font', this would have resulted in a completely different effect: the focus would be purely on passivity. However, when he says 'Nor waves the cypress' and 'Nor winks the gold fin', we cannot read this without envisioning the wave and the wink, the actions that are momentarily suspended. There is a pause, a moment of sleep, but the world is soon going to awaken: action is implicit within the passive state of the objects described.

Similarly, speaker and auditor, male and female, alternately assume the active and passive roles. The third stanza identifies the earth, lying open to the stars and waiting to be entered, with the woman, whose heart lies open, waiting to receive the male speaker. Here female is equated with passive, and male with active. However, in the next couplet the roles change: The silent meteor which is **metaphorically** associated with a plough and leaves, 'A shining furrow', is not only active but surely also a masculine image, yet this meteor is associated with the woman whose thoughts will similarly leave her mark in him. In addition, the image of the meteor as plough effects an undermining of the distinction between earth and air, while the idea that thoughts can create a 'furrow' blends the abstract with the concrete.

How do ideas of penetration and infolding, passivity and activity, become further complicated by the final stanza? The feminine lily 'slips' into the 'bosom of the lake', which lies open for the lily to penetrate – although the word 'slip' certainly undercuts any sense of harshness – and she is urged to fold herself, 'slip / Into my bosom and be lost in me'. How do you respond to those final words? Tucker suggests that the 'persuasive rhetorical power' of the lyric 'arises from the assumption that selflessness is what the self most deeply craves' (p. 370). If we do assume that the speaker is male and the one addressed female, then is it perhaps problematic that it is she who is encouraged to lose herself, while he remains 'me'? On the other hand, should we actually have made such an assumption to begin with? Conventionally the speaker of a *carpe diem* poem might be male. But is there any evidence in the actual poem to suggest that this particular speaker is male, or is Tennyson making any such clear identifications problematic? If all is blended and merged in this lyric, with all oppositions ultimately undermined and blurred, perhaps we should not make assumptions on the basis of tradition and convention and not be too hasty to assign specific sexual identities to either speaker or auditor.

TEXT 2   DARK HOUSE, BY WHICH ONCE MORE I STAND
         (from IN MEMORIAM, VII)

Dark house, by which once more I stand
  Here in the long unlovely street,
  Doors where my heart was used to beat
So quickly, waiting for a hand,

> A hand that can be clasp'd no more –
> Behold me, for I cannot sleep,
> And like a guilty thing I creep
> At earliest morning to the door.
>
> He is not here; but far away
> The noise of life begins again,
> And ghastly thro' the drizzling rain
> On the bald streets breaks the blank day.

This is one of the bleakest **lyrics** in Tennyson's *In Memoriam*, the **elegy** that he wrote after the death of his friend Hallam (see also Commentaries). Although placed early in the sequence, it was one of the last to be composed, possibly as late as 1850. As Tennyson began writing the lyrics for this sequence in 1833, the year Hallam died, this is a clear indication of the intensity of his mourning for Hallam and of the degree to which the dead man continued to haunt him. And this is quite appropriate, because above all this is a poem about a haunting.

Just before dawn, the speaker, unable to sleep, goes and stands by his dead friend's house. Here he had previously been received with warmth. Now the house is silent and dark. The speaker's description of himself as being 'like a guilty thing' echoes the description of the ghost in Shakespeare's *Hamlet*: 'And then it started like a guilty thing' (I.1.148). In much the same way as the ghost of Hamlet's father, the speaker slips away at the coming of dawn. In a striking reversal of the haunting motif, it is the speaker, the mourner, who appears like the restless ghost and not the dead man. When the speaker says 'Dark house, by which once more I stand' (line 1), it seems likely that he is not just contrasting his visit now with previous visits when the speaker is alive, but also suggesting he has been repeatedly visiting, compulsively haunting the site, since Hallam's death. And yet there is nothing there to find. The house is dark because it is night, but also because the house is, like Hallam, a body from which the spirit has gone – that is, Hallam is no longer here. Other texts are often echoed in this lyric, and **intertextuality** can be seen as another kind of haunting. It is also a way of establishing connections, and it is precisely connection that the speaker desires and yet cannot find when he haunts the dark house. The reference to the 'guilty thing' recalls not just *Hamlet* but also Wordsworth's 'Intimations of

Immortality from Recollections of Early Childhood' (1807): 'our mortal Nature / Did tremble like a guilty Thing surprised' (stanza 9). Given that Tennyson constantly searches throughout the sequence for some evidence of immortality, some evidence that he will ultimately be reunited with the dead Hallam, this echo is particularly telling. Wordsworth's **ode** explores the intensity of childhood experience as evidence of pre-existence and immortality. While 'Heaven lies about us in our infancy', however, as we mature we lose this vision and 'At length the man perceives it die away / And fade into the light of common day' (stanza 5). The speaker has no visionary experience in this poem, but equally abhors the breaking of the 'blank day'. There is also an important biblical **allusion** in this poem. Stanza 3, in beginning with a conclusive 'He is not here', echoes the words of the angel to the women who come to the tomb of Christ in order to anoint the body, 'He is not here, but is risen' (Luke 24:6). Throughout *In Memoriam* links are made between Hallam and Christ. By the end of the sequence, Christ, addressed in the Prologue as 'Strong son of God, immortal Love' (line 1) has become basically indistinguishable from Hallam, that 'noble type / Appearing ere the times were ripe, / That friend of mine who lives in God' (Epilogue, lines 138–40).

At this stage, however, there is no indication that the sequence will end quite so optimistically. While Tennyson may seek to establish connections on a verbal level with his allusions, between him and the dead man there is no connection at all. The desire for touch, for some tactile connection, is forcefully suggested by the way Tennyson manipulates the image of the hand. The hand is used over forty times in the overall sequence in order to convey, **synecdochally**, the loss of Hallam's physical presence. Throughout *In Memoriam* it is the loss of this touch which is most passionately felt. Although this lyric is in three stanzas, it tends to fall into two parts, with the first stanza run on into the second and the two linked by the repeated reference to the hand and the sad echo when 'once more' (line 1) turns into 'no more' (line 5). The second stanza is then closed by the full stop, effectively setting the two stanzas off against the third, which opens with the flat four monosyllables, 'He is not here' (line 9), which are so evocative of total loss. And yet while there is a formal linkage of stanzas one and two through repetition and echo, there is no linking of hands. As John

Rosenberg observes, 'The outstretched "hand" that closes the first stanza awaits, but never clasps, the hand that opens the second, a gulf of white space keeping them forever apart' ('Stopping for Death: Tennyson's *In Memoriam, Victorian Poetry* 30. 3–4, 1992, p. 297). Rosenberg also suggest how 'the tactile "clasp'd" of line 5 reaches forward to "Behold me" of line 6, disclosing, in addition to the imperative sense of "Look at me", the imploring sense of "hold me"'. It is not until 'Doors, where my heart was used to beat' (CXIX), a companion poem to 'Dark house', that the two men do seem to join when 'in my thoughts with scarce a sigh / I take the pressure of thine hand' (lines 11–12). (A comparison of these companion poems would reveal numerous other connections with a difference that demonstrates how the speaker's attitude has changed by this point.)

For the speaker, the bleakness of the house becomes reproduced in the dismal empty street in the 'ghastly' daybreak. How does stanza three manage to convey the speaker's withdrawal from life? Why, for example, does he refer to the 'noise' of life, and not, say, the sounds of life? The word 'noise' connotes a lack of harmony, and for the speaker, in his grief, the start of day offers nothing but a renewal of noise. Water, traditionally associated with fertility and renewal and life, is represented only by 'the drizzling rain'. What effects are created by that strikingly **alliterative** final line: 'On the bald street breaks the blank day'. The alliteration may suggest balance and regularity, but the metre here is irregular and awkward, reinforcing the lack of harmony in the scene. Darkness gives way to light, but all the light reveals is the ghastliness of the scene. It will only be later, when the speaker experiences some mystical union with Hallam in a trance-like state, that the retreat of darkness will be celebrated with joy as the wind announces the arrival of 'The dawn, the dawn' and there is a broadening 'into boundless day' (XCV, see Commentaries). For now, there is only distance and discord.

TEXT 3   I HATE THE DREADFUL HOLLOW BEHIND THE LITTLE WOOD (from *MAUD*, PART I.I. STANZAS 1–5)

i

I hate the dreadful hollow behind the little wood,
Its lips in the field above are dabbled with blood-red heath,

The red-ribb'd ledges drip with a silent horror of blood,
And Echo there, whatever is ask'd her, answers 'Death.'

ii

For there in the ghastly pit long since a body was found,
His who had given me life – O father! O God! was it well? –
Mangled, and flatten'd, and crush'd, and dinted into the ground:
There yet lies the rock that fell with him when he fell.

iii

Did he fling himself down? who knows? for a vast speculation had fail'd,
And ever he mutter'd and madden'd, and ever wann'd with despair,
And out he walk'd when the wind like a broken worldling wail'd,
And the flying god of the ruin'd woodlands drove thro' the air.

iv

I remember the time, for the roots of my hair were stirr'd
By a shuffled step, by a dead weight trail'd, by a whisper'd fright.
And my pulses closed their gates with a shock on my heart as I heard
The shrill-edged shriek of a mother divide the shuddering night.

v

Villainy somewhere! whose? One says, we are villains all.
Not he: his honest fame should at least by me be maintained:
But that old man, now lord of the broad estate and the Hall,
Dropt off gorged from a scheme that had left us flaccid and drain'd.

When *Maud* was first published, many critics associated the speaker with Tennyson himself. Such biographical connections irritated Tennyson immensely, although he was able to see the humour in many of the accusations. When one hostile critic warned 'If an author pipe of adultery, fornication, murder and suicide, set him down as the practiser of those crimes', Tennyson was quick to reply: 'Adulterer I may be, fornicator I may be, murderer I may be, suicide I am not yet' (in John Churton Collins, *Illustrations of Tennyson*, 1891, p. 286). While we are naturally tempted to identify the speaker of *In Memoriam* with Tennyson himself (although Tennyson did object to this too), with *Maud* we are quite clearly offered a dramatised **persona**. As the subtitle tells us, *Maud* is a monodrama; instead of different speakers, we are presented with just one speaker, but with different phases of his moods. The speaker has been psychically damaged by the death of his father, which he sees as having been caused by the materialism of the age, and in particular by the old lord who benefited from the financial disasters experienced by his father. The opening five stanzas introduce us to the speaker as he recalls the death – probably suicide – of his father. What does the language in these stanzas reveal to us about the character of the speaker? We could begin by considering the effect of the extremely long lines of this opening section and the repeated use of questions and exclamations. Does the speaker appear excited, angry … perhaps slightly unbalanced? He begins with an explosive expression of emotion as he expresses his horror of the 'dreadful hollow' (line 1). As the harsh and dissonant language suggests, his mind, as a result of his childhood experience, has become obsessed with death and violence. This is quite a graphic and melodramatic description, and the building up of adjectives and verbs in such phrases as 'Mangled, and flattten'd, and crush'd, and dinted' (line 7) emphasises the speaker's horror. **Alliteration** functions in a similar fashion throughout this section, establishing sound patterns with such words as hollow, heath, horror; red-ribb'd; drip and dabbled; and, most strikingly, with the chilling 's' and 'sh' sounds in stanza iv.

The colour red in these opening stanzas is powerfully associated with death and with blood, but will soon, as the love grows between Maud and the speaker, become complicated by the end of Part I through its associations with the rose and with passion. The two **symbolic** values of red will then tend to merge for the rest of the poem. Some critics have read this opening landscape as offering a symbolic vision of the female as both womb and tomb, and suggest it indicates Tennyson's ambivalence about female power. What is particularly disturbing is the connection of violence and sexuality, and this sets us up for the linking of the two ways in which the speaker will attempt to redeem himself as a man: first, through his passion for Maud, and then through going to war. The scene might also remind us of Tennyson's notorious female Nature, 'red in tooth and claw' of *In Memoriam*, but there is a significant difference. Much of the violence in these opening images has been forced upon nature, rather than being found inherent within nature. Why should Echo 'whatever is ask'd her', answer 'Death' (line 4)? Again, female sexuality is associated with death; in the classical myth Echo was a nymph in love with Narcissus; her love unreturned, she pined away until only her voice was left. More importantly, it is again what the speaker perceives – or in this case hears – that is important: the speaker hears what he wants to hear, and he hears and sees violence and death everywhere. The inexact rhyme of 'heath' and 'Death' in a section where the rhymes are otherwise exact might also suggest that what the speaker sees in the world is to a great degree something he forces upon it. From the start the speaker projects all his own obsessions upon things or people external to him. Tennyson uses **pathetic fallacy** to suggest how the speaker sees the natural world itself partaking of the ills of society; the 'wind like a broken worldling wail'd' (line 11), and, echoing the society's emphasis on profit, 'the flying gold' – that is the leaves – 'of the ruin'd woodlands drove thro' the air' (line 12). The very world has begun to be seen in terms of commodities. Recalling his father's death, the speaker searches for meaning, echoing Hamlet's 'We are arrant knaves all' (*Hamlet* III.1.128) in his search for someone to blame: 'Villainy somewhere! whose? One says, we are villains all' (line 17). And it is the old man, who benefited from the father's downfall and who is now lord of the hall, that he believes is to blame. The father's death and the family's resulting loss of economic and social position leave the old man 'gorged' but the speaker 'flaccid and drain'd' (line 20). The language here suggests a vampiric quality to the old man. It also suggests the resulting impotence of the speaker, the loss of his social identity and his masculine identity: the desire to redeem himself as a man will become a driving concern in the poem. He is left with a sense of absence and loss, and consequently with the desire to restore and reclaim what has been lost. The rest of *Maud* will trace this attempt.

PART FIVE

BACKGROUND

TENNYSON'S LIFE & WORKS

Alfred Tennyson was born at Somersby, Lincolnshire, on 6 August 1809. He was the fourth of twelve children born to the rector George Tennyson and his wife Elizabeth. Tennyson's father had been disinherited in favour of his younger brother and the subsequent quarrel between the two families continued for many years. Subject to chronic depression and nervous disorders, George Tennyson also drank heavily and often became violent. Tennyson's brother Arthur also drank to excess and his brother Edward had to be confined to a mental institution in 1833. Tennyson understandably had a lifelong fear of, and interest in, mental illness.

He was educated at Louth Grammar school from 1816 to 1820 and then at home by his father. With his brother Charles, he published his first volume in 1827, *Poems by Two Brothers*. That same year he entered Trinity College, Cambridge. In June of 1829 Tennyson was awarded the Chancellor's Gold Medal for his prize poem, *Timbuctoo*, and in October he was elected to the undergraduate debating society, the 'Apostles,' more correctly called the Cambridge Conversazione Society. The society had been founded in 1820 by a group of undergraduates who disliked the restrictions of the university curriculum at the time and wanted to explore contemporary literature and ideas more fully. At Cambridge Tennyson became friends with Arthur Hallam, and their friendship has often been thought to constitute the most important emotional relationship of Tennyson's life. In 1830, Tennyson published his first mature volume, *Poems, Chiefly Lyrical*. His father died in March of 1831, and, partly because of the family's resulting financial problems, Tennyson left Cambridge without taking a degree. Hallam had become engaged to Tennyson's sister Emily, but in 1833, on a visit to Vienna at the age of twenty-two, he died suddenly from a brain haemorrhage. That year Tennyson began *In Memoriam*, an expression of his grief for his friend.

In 1834, Tennyson fell in love with Rosa Baring; Rosa, however, seems to have agreed with her wealthy family that Tennyson's prospects were not promising and married a richer man. Tennyson's brother

Charles married Louisa Sellwood in 1836, and this year also marked the beginning of Tennyson's love for her sister Emily, whom he had first met in 1830. In 1838 Tennyson was engaged to Emily Sellwood, but the engagement was suspended in 1840, partly for financial reasons. The two-volume *Poems* of 1842 established Tennyson's reputation as a poet, but did not sell well enough to solve his financial problems. Then in 1845 he accepted a civil list pension which he had previously twice refused; this pension he received until his death. In 1847 he published *The Princess*, a long narrative poem engaging with the question of women's rights; this later formed the basis for Gilbert and Sullivan's **satirical** opera, *Princess Ida*.

When Tennyson proposed for the second time in 1848, Emily refused him, saying that their religious beliefs were too different. In 1850, however, they finally married, and subsequently had two sons, Hallam and Lionel. That year also saw the publication of *In Memoriam*, and Tennyson, now considered by many the greatest living poet, succeeded Wordsworth as Poet Laureate. In 1853 the Tennysons moved to Farringford on the Isle of Wight. *Maud, and Other Poems* appeared in 1855 and this, along with the first four *Idylls of the King*, sold well. *Enoch Arden* and more of the *Idylls of the King* appeared during the 1860s, and Tennyson started to build a second home, in Surrey, in 1868. During the 1870s, Tennyson began writing plays. His *Queen Mary*, published in 1875, was produced by Henry Irving at the Lyceum in 1876. Further plays included *Harold*, published in 1877 but not produced until 1928, and *The Falcon*, produced at the St James Theatre in 1879. His first real stage success, however, was *The Cup* (1884), produced by Irving in 1881 with Ellen Terry in the role of the heroine. During these years, he continued publishing his poetry: *Ballads and Other Poems* (1880), *Tiresias and other Poems* (1885), *Locksley Hall Sixty Years After* (1886), and *Demeter and Other Poems* (1889). In 1883 he was awarded a barony; the following year he took his seat in the House of Lords.

Two years before his death, on the request of Thomas Edison, Tennyson recorded some of his poems, including 'The Charge of the Light Brigade'; copies made from the original wax cylinders are still available, allowing Tennyson's voice to be heard today. There are also numerous interesting photographs of Tennyson, including some by the photographer Julia Margaret Cameron, who moved to the Isle of Wight in 1860 and frequently used Tennyson and his family as subjects. In appearance, Tennyson was thought to look every inch the poet: tall, dark-skinned and handsome, with long dark wavy hair. He was a strong and vigorous man (once apparently carrying a pony round the dinner-table) and his constant pipe-smoking and daily pint of port do not seem to have done him much harm. At the age of sixty-seven he was climbing a 7,000-foot mountain. His only real weakness was extreme short sight, and by eighty he was almost blind with cataracts. After he contracted a severe rheumatic illness in 1889, however, his health deteriorated; Tennyson died in 1892 and was buried in Westminster Abbey.

HISTORICAL & LITERARY BACKGROUND

REVOLUTION & REFORM

Tennyson grew up in a world marked by almost unprecedented change, a world being transformed by the industrial revolution, by scientific discoveries and new technology, and by the undermining of all absolute values in spiritual, moral and social matters. The Victorians were acutely conscious of existing in a state of transition, conscious that they were, as Matthew Arnold wrote in 'Dover Beach', 'Wandering between two worlds, one dead, / The other powerless to be born'. Mechanised industry led to a widespread movement of the population from the country to the towns, and by the 1850s, urban dwellers accounted for more than half the population. London became the largest and richest city in the world.

Both living and working conditions in the crowded towns, however, were often horrendous, and insurrection, particularly during the time of economic depression known as the 'Hungry Forties', was feared by the middle and upper classes. There were many calls for reform, particularly parliamentary reform; the working classes recognised that their conditions would not improve until the franchise was widened, and riots broke out all over the country. While Tennyson was not in sympathy with such actions, he did support the cause itself and when the first Reform Act, passed in 1832, extended the vote, he celebrated by ringing the bells of the local church in the middle of the night.

The problems of the working classes (who accounted for seventy per cent of the population by mid century), were examined by various novelists and poets; In *Sybil* (1845), Disraeli famously has one of his characters describe the nation as being in reality 'Two nations; between whom there is no intercourse and no sympathy ... the rich and the poor'. The 'condition of England' question, as it was called, became the subject of many reports and manifestos. Friedrich Engels's influential work on the social and political conditions, *The Condition of the Working Class in England in 1844* (1845), was the first major study of the effects of industrialisation on workers, and in *The Communist Manifesto* (1848), Karl Marx claimed revolution to be the only solution. Tennyson's own concerns are evident in such poems as *Maud* and in 'Locksley Hall', where the speaker warns 'Slowly comes a hungry people, as a lion creeping nigher, / Glares at one that nods and winks behind a slowly-dying fire' (lines 135–6).

In Europe revolutionary activity did indeed erupt at mid century, effecting such countries as Sicily, France, Germany, and Italy. There were outbreaks of hostility between, among others, Sardinia and Austria, Austria and Hungary, France and Italy. The major powers were all concerned either to protect or expand their territories, and Britain, as one of these powers, inevitably became involved. The year 1854 saw the start of war in the Crimea. The Russian Tsar had claimed to have protective authority over all Christians in the Turkish empire; Europe consequently began to be anxious about Russian encroachment, and France and Britain became allies in support of Turkey. This was quite a popular war with many at home, with Britain being seen as fighting against tyranny and upholding civilised values against the barbaric invaders. Tennyson responded to the Crimean war in such poems as *Maud* and the well-known 'The Charge of the Light Brigade', a poem prompted by the news of a brave but ultimately suicidal action at Balaclava. The Indian Mutiny of 1857 elicited 'The Defence of Lucknow' from Tennyson, and in 1859, in response to one of a number of fears of French invasion, a Volunteer Force was formed, some joining in response to Tennyson's recruiting poem, 'Riflemen Form!'.

THE PRESENT & THE PAST

By the 1850s, the economic condition of Britain had greatly improved as industrialisation led to numerous advances in technology. On 1 May 1851, the opening of the Great Exhibition of the Works of Industry of All Nations (which came to be known as the Crystal Palace) heralded the start of two decades of relative prosperity. This exhibition of consumer goods and new technological inventions was a celebration of Victorian progress and, although nations throughout the known world were invited to contribute to this exhibition, it was primarily a demonstration of the supremacy of the British in matters of technology and commerce. The building of new suburbs, canals, bridges, and, most notably, railways, was changing the Victorian world. For those used to travelling by stage coach, the speed of rail travel seemed miraculous, and previously unthinkable distances could now easily be covered. The railway altered conceptions not only of space and distance but also of time. While previously variations in time between towns or villages caused few problems, what we now call 'standard' time had to be set in order to establish train schedules and eliminate the possibility of railway accidents. When the Liverpool and Manchester Railway opened in 1830, Tennyson travelled on it one night; in the darkness he did not see the wheels and assumed they ran in grooves, leading him to the strange **metaphor** in 'Locksley Hall', 'Let the great world spin for ever down the ringing grooves of change'. Communication between distant communities was helped also by the introduction of the penny post in 1840, the establishment of the first commercial telegraph line in 1844, and the first penny newspaper, *The Daily Telegraph*, in 1855.

For many, industrialisation was taking the heart out of society, and numerous writers and thinkers of the time turned to the past, in particular to the medieval age, in an attempt to find a society of stability, harmony and certainty. Even in the Crystal Palace, that glass and steel shrine to Victorian modernity and progress, at the very centre was a little medieval court designed by Augustus Pugin, a reminder of a supposedly simpler and more spiritual age. As social critics, both John Ruskin and William Morris used the Middle Ages as a model of the ideal society, demonstrating how in the pre-industrial world the individual workers played a far more integral and satisfying role than in the modern factories.

Tennyson himself frequently drew on medieval legend. This can be seen in such poems as 'The Lady of Shalott', a favourite with the Pre-Raphaelite poets and painters who themselves frequently adopted medieval themes, and, even more notably, in his *Idylls of the King*, where throughout rewriting Arthurian legend, he creates his own epic vision of Britain's imperial growth and decline.

Although both the reviewers and the reading public of the time were demanding literature that was of relevance to the Victorian present, most writers of the time repeatedly drew upon the past for their subjects. Tennyson draws not only upon the medieval world, but also on the classical world. Much of his early reading was in classical and eighteenth-century literature, and this influence is frequently apparent in his choice of subject, with his use of Greek mythology in poems like 'Ulysses', 'Tithonus', 'Oenone', and 'The Lotos-Eaters'. He also draws upon types of classical literature: the influence of Ovid's *Heroides*, for example, a series of verse letters from such abandoned women as Oenone and Dido, marked by moods of frustration and despair, can be seen not only in the obvious 'Oenone', but also in 'Mariana'.

THE CONFLICT OF SCIENCE & RELIGION

This was the age of numerous discoveries in science, and Tennyson studied such popularisations of science as Lyell's *Principles of Geology* (1830–3) and Chamber's *Vestiges of the Natural History of Creation* (1844), which, although inaccurate, offered one of the first theories of 'Progressive Development' or evolution. Geological discoveries, which convinced many that the evidence of the earth's rocks showed a story that had taken millions of years to unfold, exerted great pressure on traditional religious beliefs; certainly it was no longer possible to believe literally in the account of creation found in *Genesis*. Science was beginning to suggest that even humankind, rather than being the final and perfected work of a loving god, was just one more part of a world of change, caught up in the processes of evolution. Religious faith was being slowly eroded; as John Ruskin wrote, 'If only the Geologists would let me alone, I could do very well, but those dreadful Hammers! I hear the clink of them at the end of every cadence of the Bible verses.' Later, Darwin was to add to the evolutionary theories the idea of natural selection, which suggests that species inevitably produce random variations and that only the characteristics of beings that survive to reproduce themselves could survive. Tennyson engages with these issues most notably in *In Memoriam*, where he attempts to reconcile a continuing faith in God with new evidence concerning creation. Anticipating Darwin, whose *On the Origin of Species* appeared nearly a decade later than Tennyson's elegy, he struggles with the apparent randomness and waste and cruelty of the selection process, a process which seemed to leave no room for any belief in divine guidance and order.

With its famous image of 'Nature, red in tooth and claw', *In Memoriam* also identifies one of the most important conceptual shifts in the nineteenth century, the movement from the benevolent Nature of the Romantics early in the century to the fierce nature of Darwin. Darwin and his fellow scientists put an end to any sentimental versions of a kind Mother Nature, and the monstrous force of nature in Tennyson's *In Memoriam* forms a striking opposition to Wordsworth's 'homely nurse' of the **ode** on 'Intimations of Immortality' (1807); it is still a female nature, but one who rips and tears at her children and cries 'I care for nothing, all shall go' (LVI, line 5).

In another field of science, psychology, or 'mental physiology' as it was then called, there were further important discoveries in the area of the mind. There was a shift in the first part of the century from seeing the soul or mind as distinct from the body to seeing their connections and links. This also led to an interest in and redefinition of madness. The idea of moral insanity was introduced in 1835; this was basically the idea of madness as a deviance from socially acceptable behaviour; insanity was seen to have moral or social causes, the insane personality the construct of material conditions. It was treated, therefore, not with physical restraints but with therapy, with mental restraints. Patients would be encouraged to act in a 'normal', socially acceptable manner. Madness also came to be seen as a perversion of the feelings which could quite easily exist alongside unimpaired rational faculties, blurring boundaries between madness and sanity. An interest in madness is notable in the Spasmodic poets, who flourished from the late 1830s until around 1855, and are sometimes considered the last of the **Romantics**. Like the Romantics, they elevate the poet to the status of prophet and hero and attempt to deal with the problems of the age while also exploring the individual psychology of their frequently mad protagonists. They produced a number of very long poems, the best known of which include John Philip Bailey's *Festus* (1839) and Sydney Dobell's *Balder* (1854). The Spasmodics were thoroughly satirised and discredited by William Aytoun's parody of them in *Firmilian* (1854), and it was Aytoun who gave them their name, intending the term 'spasmodic' to indicate uncontrolled verbosity. Tennyson did admire some of their work, and his *Maud*, with its gloomy hero, its psychological violence, and its concern with the age, has been considered as belonging to this Spasmodic school.

More importantly, the new interest in psychology had much to do with the development of a psychological school of poetry and the emergence of the primary Victorian innovation in poetic form: the **dramatic monologue**. Such poets as Robert Browning in 'Porphyria's Lover' and 'Johannes Agricola' and Tennyson, in 'St Simeon Stylites' and *Maud*, were particularly fascinated by aberrant and excessive speakers. The emergence of the dramatic monologue was also in part an effect of a movement away from the Romantic emphasis on an unrestrained expression of the self, on personal feeling. It tended to undercut even the idea of an essential self in its exploration of how that self was socially and culturally constructed. Browning, in his essay on Shelley, claimed that unlike the subjective poets, such as Shelley, the objective poets, including himself, sought to reproduce things external, to draw upon the world around them rather than upon an inner vision. This movement towards the external world can even be seen in the development of the realist novel during the Victorian age. While the Romantics looked inwards in their search for an essential self and truth, the Victorians, products of a more secular and material world, had little faith in essentials or universals, and were more concerned looking outwards, with examining the ways in which identity was constructed by the time and place in which one lived. Browning's *The Ring and the Book* (1868–9), a monumental experiment in the dramatic monologue, twice as long as Milton's *Paradise Lost*, offers numerous recountings of a Roman murder story from a variety of positions, questioning the very nature of truth itself. A scientific and rational age, in which society, rather than the individual, was prioritised, tended to devalue the importance of individual perceptions, and there was an accompanying devaluation of the Romantic lyric. This is not to say, however, that Victorian poets did not express intensely private experience: *In Memoriam* is clearly one of the most intensely confessional of all poems, even if this self-expression is combined with a concern with the more generally relevant issue of faith and doubt.

MEN & WOMEN

A constant rethinking of accepted ideas characterises the Victorian age, and this can also be seen with respect to gender roles. Domestic ideology, as formulated by such writers as Sarah Stickney Ellis in *The Women of England: Their Social Duties and Domestic Habits* (1839), had set out a theory of 'separate spheres' of activity for middle-class men and women. It was considered 'natural' that men should dominate the public spheres of government and commerce, science and scholarship, while women, weaker and more childlike, emotional creatures, should remain firmly placed within the domestic sphere. Here they were to be protected from the evils of the world, to fulfil their 'natural' destiny as mothers, and to exert a moral influence upon men. Two of the best known expressions of this ideology can be found in Coventry Patmore's famous long poem *The Angel in the House* (1854–62), and John Ruskin's essay 'Of Queen's Gardens' (1865). By the 1840s, however, this conventional view of gender roles had already begun to be questioned and the place of women in society to be debated. The call for redefined roles for women was frequently found in Victorian poetry, most notably perhaps in Elizabeth Barrett Browning's *Aurora Leigh* (1857), a novel in verse which made strong claims for women's social and artistic equality. Tennyson was among the first to explore the 'woman question'. *The Princess*, his long poem dealing with women's rights and women's education, was published one year before F.D. Maurice founded Queen's College, where women had the opportunity for some kind of education, and more than twenty years before J.S. Mill's *The Subjection of Women* (1869). His poetry reveals a wide engagement with gender-related issues, frequently blurring the boundaries of gender difference with, for example, the feminised Prince of *The Princess*. By mid century, masculinity was a much contested term. The middle-class Victorians reacted against the previous model of the leisured male aristocrat, now seen as self-indulgent and even effeminate. Thomas Carlyle's 'Captain of Industry' helped define the new ideal man in terms of achievement, as capitalist, while Charles Kingsley was instrumental in establishing ideas of muscular Christianity' or 'Christian manliness', associated with self-restraint and power. Tennyson engages with this debate in his exploration of competing definitions of masculinity in works like *Maud*, where the speaker desires to attain control over his violent emotions, and calls for new kinds of masculinity, with such figures as the ideal 'female' king Arthur of the *Idylls*. Homosexuality – the term was first coined in German during the 1880s – further complicated notions of masculinity in the late Victorian period. Although Tennyson never directly expressed sexual desire for another man, many critics today consider that his struggle to identify his feelings for Hallam in *In Memoriam*, his naming of himself as widower, bride and mother, constitute an expression of what Lord Alfred Douglas so notoriously later described as 'the Love that dare not speak its name'.

The student wishing to find out more about the Victorian age will find two works of particular value: *A Companion to Victorian Literature and Culture*, edited by Herbert F. Tucker, Blackwell, 1999, and *Victorian People and Ideas*, by Richard Altick, Norton, 1973.

PART SIX

C RITICAL HISTORY & FURTHER READING

R ECEPTION & EARLY CRITICAL REVIEWS

Although Arthur Hallam and others in Tennyson's circle of friends wrote enthusiastic reviews, Tennyson's first volume, *Poems, Chiefly Lyrical* (1830), was not well received by all. Christopher North, in *Blackwood's*, attacked both the friendly critics and the 'distinguished silliness' of a group of poems he thought undeserving of favourable attention, but, although he believed Tennyson had 'small power over the common feelings and thoughts of men' (Jump, p. 52), he had to concede that Tennyson was indeed a poet, and one of 'fine faculties' (Jump, p. 63). Response to the second volume, *Poems* (published at the end of 1832, but dated 1833), was even less favourable, with Tennyson accused of affectation and obscurity. J.W. Croker, the critic who had been accused of destroying Keats with the savagery of his criticism, made a similar attempt to demolish Tennyson. The brutal ridicule of his review in the influential *Quarterly Review* (popularly known as the 'Hang, draw, and quarterly' because of its generally harsh reviews) seriously damaged Tennyson's morale and managed to restrict the sale of the volume over the next two years to 200 out of the 450 which were printed. Tennyson did not attempt publication again until 1842. The two-volume *Poems*, which included some previous work extensively revised, showed that Tennyson had in fact paid some attention to the criticisms. The *Quarterly* changed its mind about him, and many of his contemporaries considered this edition demonstrated a great poetic talent. Nevertheless, praise was still qualified; John D. Jump observes that 'Tennyson was being pressed to write a long poem, to handle an important contemporary subject, to display more human sympathy, and to inculcate sound doctrine' (p. 6). *The Princess* was a response to these demands, but although some critics considered this new poem to capture the modern age, others thought it showed little advance. It was *In Memoriam* that turned Tennyson into an important public figure and established him in the eyes of many as the greatest poet of the age. *In Memoriam* was an immediate critical and popular success; reviews were almost entirely favourable and 5,000 copies sold within a matter of weeks. *Maud* (1855), however, although the sales were good, was considered morbid and obscure, with one hostile reviewer suggesting there was one too many vowels in the title, and that it would make sense no matter which was deleted. Most reviewers, like Peter Bayne, looked upon *Maud* as a 'passing variation' (Jump, p. 10), and were far more impressed by the *Idylls of the King*, four of which had appeared in 1859. Walter Bagehot, for example, questioned *Maud*, which he associated with a certain unhealthiness of the imagination, but considered the *Idylls* to show 'the delicate grace of a very composed genius' and 'the trace of a very mature judgement' in every line (Jump, p. 219). Tennyson's reputation reached its heights in the 1860s and he was widely hailed as the greatest poet of the age. *Enoch Arden* (1864) was immensely popular and gained Tennyson an even wider public audience. For the rest of his life, Tennyson's position was assured, and, although there were a few ominous signs that tastes were changing, for his contemporaries Tennyson remained the 'Master Poet' (Jump, p. 445).

WORKS CITED
John D. Jump, ed., *Tennyson: The Critical Heritage*, Routledge, 1967

THE PUBLIC & PRIVATE POET

In 1870, the poet Alfred Austin, who was to succeed Tennyson as Laureate, asked:

> Can anybody in his senses imagine posterity speaking of our age as the age of Tennyson? Posterity will be too kind to do anything so sardonic. It will speak of it as the age of Railways, the age of Destructive Criticism, or the age of Penny Papers. In some way or other it will try to distinguish us. But the age of Tennyson! The notion is, of course, preposterous. (Jump, p. 310).

For Edwardian critics in the decade after Tennyson's death, however, what was 'Victorian' and what was 'Tennysonian' were virtually synonymous; he had indeed come to represent his age. The association was not favourable to Tennyson's reputation. There was a strong reaction against Victorianism and, inevitably therefore, a strong reaction against

Tennyson. There were those who looked back nostalgically to Victorian values of home and empire who continued to admire Tennyson, but they were in the minority. The modernist writers, trying to break with the past, misread Tennyson in order to make him into the embodiment of all the problems they identified in Victorian writing: empty **rhetoric**, insistent morality and sentimentality, and verbosity. They constructed a sadly simplified Victorianism against which they could define themselves as new and different. It became fashionable, even a sign of discriminating intelligence, to sneer at Tennyson. Harold Nicolson's *Tennyson: Aspects of his Life, Character and Poetry* was an influential early attempt to reassert the importance of Tennyson, but ultimately only further confused our understanding of the poet. Nicolson argued for the need to distinguish the private from the public poet, suggesting that Tennyson was naturally a subjective and lyric poet, and that he was transformed by his age, by the demands of his critics and his laureateship, into the didactic poet and spokesman of Victorian values. This image of a Tennyson split between the public and private persisted throughout much of the twentieth century. W.H. Auden notoriously argued that he had the finest ear of any English poet but was also the stupidest. At best, for much of this century, Tennyson was considered a gifted lyric poet whose literary career had been ruined by the demands of the age and his attempt to speak of public, historical issues. A gradually less biased and more searching account of Tennyson emerged during the 1950s. E.D.H. Johnson in *The Alien Vision of Victorian Poetry* (1952) suggested that Tennyson, and most of his fellow poets, were in fact at odds with their age. Johnson believed that these poets had what he calls a double awareness, an ability to cater to the demands of their society while also incorporating different and frequently contradictory insights. Rather than seeing Tennyson as offering banal moral lessons, he suggested that Tennyson was showing the incompatibility between the world and man's inner visions of the world. Jerome Buckley's *Tennyson: The Growth of a Poet* traced the development of Tennyson as a poet partly to attack the private/public division, and to offer a more synthesised view of the poet's work. The oversimplified and misleading view of a dual Tennyson was most effectively corrected, however, in the 1960s. John Killham's collection of essays marked a real turning point in the rehabilitation of Tennyson' reputation: as Killham observed, rather than subscribing to the notion of two Tennysons, 'one would object much less to the idea of twenty Tennysons' (p. 8). During the late 1950s and 1960s, critics also began to reconsider many of Tennyson's neglected works, and a number of significant specialised studies began to appear, including John R. Reed's *Perception and Design in Tennyson's 'Idylls of the King'* (1969) and Ralph Rader's *Tennyson's Maud* (1963). John Killham's groundbreaking *Tennyson and 'The Princess'* (1958) contextualised the poem, examining Tennyson's engagement with the feminist controversy and evolutionary discoveries, while *In Memoriam* was the focus of John Dixon Hunt's casebook of essays, and Alan Sinfield's still unmatched study of its language (1971).

WORKS CITED

Jerome Hamilton Buckley, *Tennyson. The Growth of a Poet*, Harvard University Press, 1961

John Dixon Hunt, *Tennyson. In Memoriam. A Casebook*, Macmillan, 1970

E.D.H. Johnson, The *Alien Vision of Victorian Poetry*, Princeton University Press, 1952

John D. Jump, ed., *Tennyson: The Critical Heritage*, Routledge, 1967

John Killham, ed., *Critical Essays on the Poetry of Tennyson*, Routledge, 1960

John Killham, *Tennyson and 'The Princess'*, Athlone Press, 1958

Harold Nicolson, *Tennyson, Aspects of His Life, Character and Poetry*, Constable, 1923

Ralph Wilson Rader, *Tennyson's Maud: The Biographical Genesis*, University of California Press, 1963

John R. Reed, *Perception and Design in Tennyson's 'Idylls of the King'*, Ohio University Press, 1969

Alan Sinfield, *The Language of Tennyson's 'In Memoriam'*, Blackwell, 1971

FURTHER READING
Elizabeth A. Francis, ed., *Tennyson. A Collection of Critical Essays*,
Prentice Hall, 1980
Collection of essays from the 1960s and 1970s

Christopher Ricks, *Tennyson*, Macmillan, 1972
A bio-critical study

TENNYSON TODAY

Over the last twenty years, as we have begun to discover more about the complexities of the Victorian age, Tennyson's close association with his times has served him well, leading to a further revival of critical interest in his work. Rebecca Stott recalls Thackeray's comment that Tennyson 'reads all sorts of things, swallows and digests them like a great poetical boa-constrictor' and then observes that 'it seems at times as if Tennyson has swallowed what we have come to call the Victorian Age, or that his poetry is a fossil which enables us to observe with twentieth-century critical apparatus all the complex sinews and musculature of that age' (p. 1). Similarly, Eve Sedgwick suggests that Tennyson seems like 'a Christmas present to the twentieth-century student of ideology' (in Stott, p. 182). Tennyson is no longer seen as a simple spokesperson for the values of his age, however, but as a poet revealing numerous ideological tensions. It is not surprising, therefore, that he has become of most interest to critics in the fields of cultural studies and feminist theory.

The special issue of *Victorian Poetry* devoted to Tennyson in 1992 demonstrates the wide variety of ways in which critics are resituating his work within its historical and political contexts. For example, Matthew Rowlinson examines the colonialist backdrop of 'Ulysses'; Ian McGuire examines the imperialist theme in the *Idylls of the King*; Carl Plasa offers a feminist reading of 'The Lady of Shalott'; and Linda Shires considers the construction of masculinities in Tennyson (all in Joseph ed., *Victorian Poetry*). Herbert Tucker's *Critical Essays on Alfred Lord Tennyson* (1993), a collection of essays drawn from the 1980s, and Rebecca Stott's *Tennyson* (1996) provide further evidence that gender continues to be one of the most important areas of exploration in Tennyson studies. Two particularly notable essays in Stott's collection are Joseph Bristow's 'Nation, Class and Gender: Tennyson's *Maud* and War' in which he examines competing ideas about masculinity and the tension between being a poet and being a man in an age when poetry was becoming feminised, and Eve Sedgwick's 'Tennyson's *Princess*: One Bride for Seven Brothers' which examines the poem's concern with the patriarchal homosocial bonding which places women as objects of exchange between men. In Tucker's collection, the groundbreaking essay by Elliot Gilbert examines Tennyson's treatment of King Arthur as the 'female king', as exemplifying the growing assertion of female authority in the Victorian age, and showing how the female energy of myth and nature substitutes for the male energy of culture and history. Also in Tucker, Christopher Craft traces the encoded and diffused expression of homosexual desire in *In Memoriam*. The Stott and Tucker collections also provide significant essays in cultural studies, including, in Stott, Gerhard K. Joseph on the alienation of work in 'The Lady of Shalott' and Alan Sinfield on the cultural politics of prophesy. These two collections of essays will provide the reader with an excellent sample of recent approaches to Tennyson. Other important books on Tennyson in recent years include Alan Sinfield's influential **Cultural materialist** reading which sees Tennyson as engaged in a struggle with the dominant ideas of his time; Matthew Rowlinson's Lacanian *Tennyson's Fixations: Psychoanalysis and the Topics of the Early Poetry* (1994) and Donald Hair's *Tennyson's Language* (1991) which draw upon language theory to illuminate Tennyson's own thinking about language as revealed in his poems.

WORKS CITED

Donald S. Hair, *Tennyson's Language*, University of Toronto Press, 1991

Gerhard K. Joseph, ed. Special centenary issue on Tennyson, *Victorian Poetry*, 30.3–4, 1992

Matthew Rowlinson, *Tennyson's Fixations: Psychoanalysis and the Topics of the Early Poetry*, University Press of Virginia, 1994

Alan Sinfield, *Alfred Tennyson*, Blackwell, 1986

Rebecca Stott, ed., *Tennyson*, Addison Wesley Longman, 1996

Herbert Tucker, ed., *Critical Essays on Alfred Lord Tennyson*, G.K. Hall, 1993

FURTHER READING

Harold Bloom, ed., *Alfred Lord Tennyson* 1985

Another useful collection of essays

Philip Collins, ed. *Tennyson: Seven Essays*, St Martin's Press, 1992

Includes essays on biographical, social and critical issues

Marion Shaw, *Alfred Lord Tennyson*, Humanities Press, 1988

A feminist approach with some particularly interesting discussions of masculinity

Herbert Tucker, *Tennyson and the Doom of Romanticism*, Harvard University Press, 1988

One of the best books on Tennyson, with brilliant readings of a wide selection of the poems

World events	Author's life	Literary events
1809 Beethoven writes Piano Concerto No 5	**1809** Alfred Tennyson born, 4th son of clergyman, Lincolnshire	
1811 Prince of Wales becomes Regent		
1812 Napoleon retreats from Moscow		**1812** Robert Browning born
	1816-20 Attends Louth Grammar School	**1816** Samuel Taylor Coleridge, *Christabel*, 'Kubla Khan'
		1819 Lord Byron, *Don Juan*
1820 Death of George III; accession of George IV		
		1821 Death of John Keats
	1827 Alfred and Charles Tennyson, *Poems by Two Brothers*; enters Trinity College, Cambridge	
	1829 Becomes friends with Arthur Hallam; wins prize for 'Timbuctoo'; becomes member of the Apostles	
1830 Death of George IV; accession of William IV; Lyell's *Principles of Geology*	**1830** *Poems, Chiefly Lyrical*	**1830** Emily Dickinson born
		1830-55 fl. Spasmodic Poets
	1831 Tennyson's father dies; leaves Cambridge	
1832 Reform Bill	**1832** Tours Rhine with Hallam	
	1833 Hallam dies	
	1836 Falls in love with Emily Sellwood	
1837 Death of William IV; accession of Queen Victoria		
1838 Formation of Anti-Corn-Law League		
		1839 John Philip Bailey, *Festus*
	1840 Breaks off engagement to Emily	
	1842 *Poems*	
1844 Chamber's *Vestiges of the Natural History of Creation*		

World events	Author's life	Literary events
1845 Friedrich Engels, *The Condition of the Working Class in England*; famine in Ireland	**1845** Granted Civil List pension	**1845** Benjamin Disraeli, *Sybil*
	1847 *The Princess*	
1848 Karl Marx, *The Communist Manifesto*; revolutions in Paris, Berlin, Vienna, Venice, Rome, Milan, Naples, Prague and Budapest; formation of Pre-Raphaelite Brotherhood		
	1849 Renews friendship with Emily	
	1850 *In Memoriam*; marries Emily; appointed Poet Laureate	**1850** William Wordsworth dies
1851 The Great Exhibition		
	1852 His son Hallam born	
	1853 Moves to the Isle of Wight	**1853** Matthew Arnold, *Poems*
1854 Outbreak of Crimean War	**1854** His son Lionel born	**1854** Sydney Dobell, *Balder*; William Aytoun, *Firmilian*; Coventry Patmore begins *The Angel in the House*
1855 First publication of *Daily Telegraph*	**1855** *Maud*	**1855** Walt Whitman, *Leaves of Grass*
1856 Crimean War ends		**1856** Victor Hugo, *Les Consolations*
1857 The Indian Mutiny		**1857** Elizabeth Barrett Browning, *Aurora Leigh*; Charles Baudelaire, *Les Fleurs du Mal*
		1858 William Morris, *The Defence of Guenevere*
1859 Charles Darwin, *On the Origin of Species*	**1859** *Idylls of the King*	
1861-5 American Civil War		
	1862 Audience with Queen	

World events	Author's life	Literary events
	1864 Enoch Arden	
		1865 John Ruskin, 'Of Queen's Gardens'
		1866 Algernon Charles Swinburne, Poems and Ballads
1867 Nobel patents dynamite		
		1868-9 Browning, The Ring and the Book
	1869 Holy Grail and Other Poems	**1869** J.S. Mill, The Subjection of Women
1870-1 Franco-Prussian War		
	1872 Works	
1874 Disraeli becomes PM; first Impressionist Exhibition		
	1875-92 Plays: Queen Mary, Harold, The Cup and the Falcon, Becket, The Promise of May, The Foresters	
1880 Gladstone PM; Wagner, Parsifal	**1880** Ballads and Other Poems	
	1883 Accepts barony	**1883** George Meredith, Poems and Lyrics of the Joy of Earth
	1885 Tiresias and Other Poems	
	1886 Death of Lionel; Locksley Hall Sixty Years After	
1887 Queen Victoria's Golden Jubilee		
1888 Jack the Ripper murders six women		
	1889 Demeter and Other Poems	**1889** W.B. Yeats, Crossways
		1890 Robert Bridges, Shorter Poems
	1892 Dies	
		1893 Francis Thompson, 'The Hound of Heaven'

alexandrine a line of twelve syllables; the nearest English equivalent is the iambic hexameter. It is used at the end of each of the opening stanzas in 'The Lotos-Eaters'

alliteration a sequence of repeated consonantal sounds in a stretch of language. The matching consonants are usually at the beginning of words or are stressed syllables. Tennyson plays on 'm' and 'w' when the speaker in *Maud* describes his father: 'And ever he mutter'd and madden'd, and ever wann'd with despair, / And out he walk'd when the wind like a broken worlding wail'd'

allusion a reference in a work of literature to something outside itself. Tennyson alludes to Hamlet's ghost when he describes himself 'like a guilty thing' in *In Memoriam*, VII

ambiguity the capacity of words and sentences to have double, multiple, or uncertain meanings

anapest a trisyllabic metrical foot consisting of two unstressed syllables followed by a stressed syllable. Tennyson begins with anapests in this line from 'Locksley Hall': 'In the Spring a young man's fancy lightly turns to thoughts of love'

anaphora a rhetorical device in which a word or phrase is repeated in several successive clauses. See for example the use of anaphora to stress the climactic moment when the Lady of Shalott looks out upon the world: 'She left the web, she left the loom, / She made three paces thro' the room, / She saw the water-lily bloom, / She saw the helmet and the plume'

apostrophe rhetorical term for a speech addressed to a person, idea or thing. Tennyson uses this device in the final line of 'Tears, idle tears': 'O Death in Life, the days that are no more'

assonance the correspondence, or near correspondence, in the stressed vowel of two or more words. Assonance is used in Mariana's refrain as she repeats how all is 'dreary' and she 'aweary'

blank verse unrhymed iambic pentameter: a line of five iambs. One of the commonest of English metres and used by Tennyson in such poems as 'Ulysses' and 'Oenone'

caesura a pause within a line of verse. In this example from *In Memoriam*, section VII, the caesura emphasises the flatness of life without Hallam: 'He is not here;

but far away / The noise of life begins again'. The caesura is followed by an enjambed line

carpe diem (Lat: 'seize the day') the tag denotes a theme or subject common in literature, especially lyric verse: the invitation to enjoy youth and life quickly, before the onset of dull maturity. Tennyson's 'Come down, O maid' is written in this tradition

Cultural materialism draws attention to and exposes the process by which ideology presents power relations as harmonious and coherent; texts are understood as 'cultural interventions', promoting a particular view of reality within a specific historical condition. The values within the text are shown to be not 'universal', but constructions made by others within particular circumstances. The text is the site of struggle over meaning which is always political

elegy a poem of lamentation, concentrating on the death of a single person, like *In Memoriam*. **pastoral elegy** the pastoral tradition originated with the Greek idylls of Theocritus in the third century BC. Nature mourns the death of the person who is being celebrated and there are fixed conventions, including the lament of all nature, the procession of mourners, the contrast between the fixity of death and the reawakening of spring

end-stopped the end of a line of verse coincides with an essential grammatical pause usually signalled by punctuation. Arthur's famous lines in the 'Morte d'Arthur' are end-stopped: 'The old order changeth, yielding place to new, / And God fulfils Himself in many ways, / Lest one good custom should corrupt the world'

enjambment the running over of the sense and grammatical structure from one verse line or stanza to the next without a punctuated pause. Enjambment is used in the description of the cry of the queens in the 'Morte d'Arthur' which is 'an agony / Of lamentation, like a wind, that shrills / All night in a waste land'

epic a long narrative poem in elevated style, about the exploits of superhuman heroes. Tennyson's 'Morte d'Arthur' is in the style of an epic

epigraph an inscription, or fragments or quotations placed at the beginning of a literary work

epistolary written in the form of a letter

epithalamion a poem celebrating a marriage, traditionally sung outside the bedroom of the newly weds. Tennyson's *In Memoriam* finishes with a description of a wedding that suggests this form

epithet an adjective, or adjectival phrase, which defines a special quality or attribute. In 'Morte d'Arthur', Bedivere is repeatedly described with the epithet 'bold': 'the bold sir Bedivere'

euphony language which sounds pleasantly smooth and musical. The opening of 'The Lotos-Eaters' is a striking example

feminist criticism within feminist criticism there are numerous different positions. One of the main tenets of feminist thought is that male ways of perceiving and ordering are inscribed into the prevailing ideology of society and into language itself. Many feminist critics argue that patriarchal culture is marked by the urge to define, categorise and control, and that it subjects thought to binary systems of irreconcilable opposites. Language is phallogocentric; that is, it privileges the male and subordinates the female. Femininity is therefore considered a construction of society and of language. Sexual identity, what we are born with, becomes distinct from gender, which would include those traits we are encouraged to acquire and those traits which are assigned by phallogocentric language. Both masculinity and femininity are constructs. The difference is, feminists might argue, men are in control of the definitions

ghazal short Persian lyric, using a single final word at regular intervals to produce a form of rhyme and focusing on amatory matters, using a series of standard images, such as the rose, stars, cypresses

iambic hexameter a line of six iambic feet

iambic pentameter an iambic foot has an unstressed followed by a stressed syllable; a pentameter has five feet; an iambic pentameter is therefore scanned as -/-/-/-/-/. An example from 'Ulysses' would be 'To strive, to seek, to find, and not to yield'

idyll a short poem describing a picturesque rustic scene or incident

in medias res (Lat. 'in the middle of things'). A phrase describing a common technique of story-telling in which the narrator begins in the middle of a story or action. Tennyson's 'Morte d'Arthur' begins in this way: 'So all day long the noise of battle roll'd'

irony saying one thing while meaning another

Marxist criticism criticism that considers literature in relation to its capacity to reflect the struggle between the classes

metaphor goes further than a comparison between two different things or ideas by fusing them together. A metaphor has two different parts: the *tenor* is the subject of the metaphoric comparison, while the *vehicle* is the metaphoric word which carries over its meaning. Night is metaphorically described as a 'black bat' in 'Come into the garden, Maud'. Night is the tenor, while black bat is the vehicle. Tennyson's metaphors are often *implicit* rather than *explicit*: that is, the tenor must be assumed

metre verse is distinguished from prose because it contains some linguistic element which is repeated, creating a sense of pattern. In English verse the commonest pattern is stress- or accent-based metre, which consists of the regular arrangement of strong stresses in a stretch of language

monologue a single person speaking, with or without an audience, is uttering a monologue. The **dramatic monologue** refers to a specific kind of poem in which a single person, not the poet, is speaking, usually to a specific auditor, and usually in a specific dramatic situation. Tennyson and Browning developed this form almost simultaneously

ode a form of lyric poem characterised by its length, intricate stanza forms, grandeur of style and seriousness of purpose. Tennyson wrote many odes, including an 'Ode on the Death of the Duke of Wellington'

onomatopoeia words which sound like the noise they describe. Tennyson's final lines in 'Come down, O maid' are frequently cited for their effective onomatopoeic effects: 'The moan of doves in immemorial elms, / And murmuring of innumerable bees'

oxymoron a figure of speech in which contradictory terms are brought together in what is at first sight an impossible combination, for example 'sweet sorrow'

paradox an apparently self-contradictory statement; yet lying behind the apparent absurdity is meaning or truth

parallelism the building up of a sentence or statement using repeated syntactic units. Parallelism achieves an effect of balance

parody an imitation of a specific work of literature, designed to mock

pathetic fallacy used to describe the assumption of an equation between their own mood and the world about them; nature can be specifically described in terms of one's feelings. In the opening of *Maud*, the speaker's description of the 'red-ribb'd ledges' which 'drip with a silent horror of blood' clearly relates to his own horror

persona many poems are spoken by a speaker who is clearly not the author. In *Maud*, for example, the speaker is not named, but it is clearly not Tennyson

personification a variety of figurative or metaphorical language in which things or ideas are treated as if they were human beings. In 'Mariana', personification is used in the images of the sluice that 'slept' and the 'wooing wind'

Post-structuralism systems of criticism that build on and refine the network of ideas known as structuralism, a basic tenet of which is that meaning is not inherent in words but depends on their mutual relationships within the system of language, a system that is based on differences

Pre-Raphaelite a group of artists in the mid Victorian age, including John Millais, Holman Hunt and Dante Gabriel Rossetti, who aimed to return to the truthfulness and simplicity of medieval art. They admired Tennyson's work, and painted scenes from such poems as 'The Lady of Shalott' and 'Mariana'

quatrain a stanza of four lines

refrain words or lines repeated in the course of a poem, recurring at intervals, sometimes with slight variation. In 'Oenone', the refrain is based on variations upon 'Dear mother Ida, harken ere I die'

rhetorical using the devices of rhetoric, by which an orator can help convince or sway an audience

rhyme chiming or matching sounds which create an audible sense of pattern. **end rhyme** the matching sounds come at the ends of line of verse. **internal rhyme** a pair of rhyming words within a line of verse rather than at the ends of lines. **feminine rhymes** are created when the final syllable is unstressed and the preceding stressed syllable has to chime as well as the final syllable (flying/dying). **masculine rhymes** chime on the last syllable which also bears a final stress (may/day)

romance primarily medieval fictions dealing with adventures of chivalry and love

Romanticism literature of the period from 1789 to 1830 which, among other features, such as a love of nature, shared a concern to value feeling and emotion rather than the human capacity to reason; to value the self rather than society in general; to value the 'imagination'; to aspire towards something beyond the ordinary world; and to rebel against poetic stultification and outmoded political institutions

satire literature which examines or exhibits vice or folly and makes them appear ridiculous

sibilance sibilants are 's', 'z' and 'sh' sounds, and their repetition is a particular kind of alliteration

simile a figure of speech in which one thing is said to be like another and the comparison is made with the use of 'like' or 'as'. In 'The Lady of Shalott', Lancelot's 'helmet and the helmet-feather / Burn'd like one burning flame together'. **epic simile** a long simile, sometimes over twenty lines, which typically interrupts the narrative in an epic poem, allowing the poet to make detailed comparisons

spondees a metrical foot consisting of two long syllables or two strong stresses

stanza a unit of several lines of verse. **Spenserian stanza** a form invented by Edmund Spenser for *The Fairie Queene* (1590, 1596). Eight lines of iambic pentameter followed by an alexandrine or line of twelve syllables, rhyming *ababbcbcc*. The opening of 'The Lotos-Eaters' is in Spenserian stanzas

symbol something that represents something else, especially a material object representing an abstract idea

synecdoche a figure of speech in which a part is used to describe the whole of things

tone in conveying tone, words can suggest the sense of a particular manner or mood in which a passage should be read

trochee, trochaic a trochee is a foot consisting of a strongly stressed syllable followed by a weakly stressed syllable. Trochaic metres are common in English poetry. Tennyson uses a trochaic line in 'Willows whiten, aspens quiver'

Glennis Byron is Senior Lecturer in English Studies at the University of Stirling. She is the author of *Letitia Landon. The Woman Behind L.E.L.* and various articles in the fields of nineteenth-century poetry and Gothic literature, and she is the editor of such works as *Dracula*, Broadview, 1997, and *Dracula. The New Casebook*, Macmillan, 1998.

York Notes Advanced

Margaret Atwood
Cat's Eye

Margaret Atwood
The Handmaid's Tale

Jane Austen
Mansfield Park

Jane Austen
Persuasion

Jane Austen
Pride and Prejudice

Alan Bennett
Talking Heads

William Blake
Songs of Innocence and of Experience

Charlotte Brontë
Jane Eyre

Emily Brontë
Wuthering Heights

Angela Carter
Nights at the Circus

Geoffrey Chaucer
The Franklin's Prologue and Tale

Geoffrey Chaucer
The Miller's Prologue and Tale

Geoffrey Chaucer
Prologue To the Canterbury Tales

Geoffrey Chaucer
The Wife of Bath's Prologue and Tale

Samuel Taylor Coleridge
Selected Poems

Joseph Conrad
Heart of Darkness

Daniel Defoe
Moll Flanders

Charles Dickens
Great Expectations

Charles Dickens
Hard Times

Emily Dickinson
Selected Poems

John Donne
Selected Poems

Carol Ann Duffy
Selected Poems

George Eliot
Middlemarch

George Eliot
The Mill on the Floss

T.S. Eliot
Selected Poems

F. Scott Fitzgerald
The Great Gatsby

E.M. Forster
A Passage to India

Brian Friel
Translations

Thomas Hardy
The Mayor of Casterbridge

Thomas Hardy
The Return of the Native

Thomas Hardy
Selected Poems

Thomas Hardy
Tess of the d'Urbervilles

Seamus Heaney
Selected Poems from Opened Ground

Nathaniel Hawthorne
The Scarlet Letter

Kazuo Ishiguro
The Remains of the Day

Ben Jonson
The Alchemist

James Joyce
Dubliners

John Keats
Selected Poems

Christopher Marlowe
Doctor Faustus

Arthur Miller
Death of a Salesman

John Milton
Paradise Lost Books I & II

Toni Morrison
Beloved

Sylvia Plath
Selected Poems

Alexander Pope
Rape of the Lock and other poems

William Shakespeare
Antony and Cleopatra

William Shakespeare
As You Like It

William Shakespeare
Hamlet

William Shakespeare
King Lear

William Shakespeare
Measure for Measure

William Shakespeare
The Merchant of Venice

William Shakespeare
A Midsummer Night's Dream

William Shakespeare
Much Ado About Nothing

William Shakespeare
Othello

William Shakespeare
Richard II

William Shakespeare
Romeo and Juliet

William Shakespeare
The Taming of the Shrew

William Shakespeare
The Tempest

William Shakespeare
Twelfth Night

William Shakespeare
The Winter's Tale

George Bernard Shaw
Saint Joan

Mary Shelley
Frankenstein

Jonathan Swift
Gulliver's Travels and A Modest Proposal

Alfred, Lord Tennyson
Selected Poems

Alice Walker
The Color Purple

Oscar Wilde
The Importance of Being Earnest

Tennessee Williams
A Streetcar Named Desire

John Webster
The Duchess of Malfi

Virginia Woolf
To the Lighthouse

W.B. Yeats
Selected Poems

Jane Austen
Emma

Jane Austen
Sense and Sensibility

Samuel Beckett
Waiting for Godot and
Endgame

Louis de Bernières
Captain Corelli's Mandolin

Charlotte Brontë
Villette

Caryl Churchill
Top Girls and *Cloud Nine*

Charles Dickens
Bleak House

T.S. Eliot
The Waste Land

Thomas Hardy
Jude the Obscure

Homer
The Iliad

Homer
The Odyssey

Aldous Huxley
Brave New World

D.H. Lawrence
Selected Poems

Christopher Marlowe
Edward II

George Orwell
Nineteen Eighty-four

Jean Rhys
Wide Sargasso Sea

William Shakespeare
Henry IV Pt I

William Shakespeare
Henry IV Part II

William Shakespeare
Macbeth

William Shakespeare
Richard III

Tom Stoppard
Arcadia and *Rosencrantz and
Guildenstern are Dead*

Virgil
The Aeneid

Jeanette Winterson
*Oranges are Not the Only
Fruit*

Tennessee Williams
Cat on a Hot Tin Roof

Metaphysical Poets

GCSE and equivalent levels

Maya Angelou
I Know Why the Caged Bird Sings

Jane Austen
Pride and Prejudice

Alan Ayckbourn
Absent Friends

Elizabeth Barrett Browning
Selected Poems

Robert Bolt
A Man for All Seasons

Harold Brighouse
Hobson's Choice

Charlotte Brontë
Jane Eyre

Emily Brontë
Wuthering Heights

Shelagh Delaney
A Taste of Honey

Charles Dickens
David Copperfield

Charles Dickens
Great Expectations

Charles Dickens
Hard Times

Charles Dickens
Oliver Twist

Roddy Doyle
Paddy Clarke Ha Ha Ha

George Eliot
Silas Marner

George Eliot
The Mill on the Floss

Anne Frank
The Diary of Anne Frank

William Golding
Lord of the Flies

Oliver Goldsmith
She Stoops To Conquer

Willis Hall
The Long and the Short and the Tall

Thomas Hardy
Far from the Madding Crowd

Thomas Hardy
The Mayor of Casterbridge

Thomas Hardy
Tess of the d'Urbervilles

Thomas Hardy
The Withered Arm and other Wessex Tales

L.P. Hartley
The Go-Between

Seamus Heaney
Selected Poems

Susan Hill
I'm the King of the Castle

Barry Hines
A Kestrel for a Knave

Louise Lawrence
Children of the Dust

Harper Lee
To Kill a Mockingbird

Laurie Lee
Cider with Rosie

Arthur Miller
The Crucible

Arthur Miller
A View from the Bridge

Robert O'Brien
Z for Zachariah

Frank O'Connor
My Oedipus Complex and Other Stories

George Orwell
Animal Farm

J.B. Priestley
An Inspector Calls

J.B. Priestley
When We Are Married

Willy Russell
Educating Rita

Willy Russell
Our Day Out

J.D. Salinger
The Catcher in the Rye

William Shakespeare
Henry IV Part 1

William Shakespeare
Henry V

William Shakespeare
Julius Caesar

William Shakespeare
Macbeth

William Shakespeare
The Merchant of Venice

William Shakespeare
A Midsummer Night's Dream

William Shakespeare
Much Ado About Nothing

William Shakespeare
Romeo and Juliet

William Shakespeare
The Tempest

William Shakespeare
Twelfth Night

George Bernard Shaw
Pygmalion

Mary Shelley
Frankenstein

R.C. Sherriff
Journey's End

Rukshana Smith
Salt on the Snow

John Steinbeck
Of Mice and Men

Robert Louis Stevenson
Dr Jekyll and Mr Hyde

Jonathan Swift
Gulliver's Travels

Robert Swindells
Daz 4 Zoe

Mildred D. Taylor
Roll of Thunder, Hear My Cry

Mark Twain
Huckleberry Finn

James Watson
Talking in Whispers

Edith Wharton
Ethan Frome

William Wordsworth
Selected Poems

A Choice of Poets

Mystery Stories of the Nineteenth Century including The Signalman

Nineteenth Century Short Stories

Poetry of the First World War

Six Women Poets

NOTES